YOU ARE FREAKING FABULOUS!

- Keep your head up.
- Be proud of yourself.
- Take your time.

THIS BOOK BELONGS TO:

____

BY PICK ME READ ME PRESS

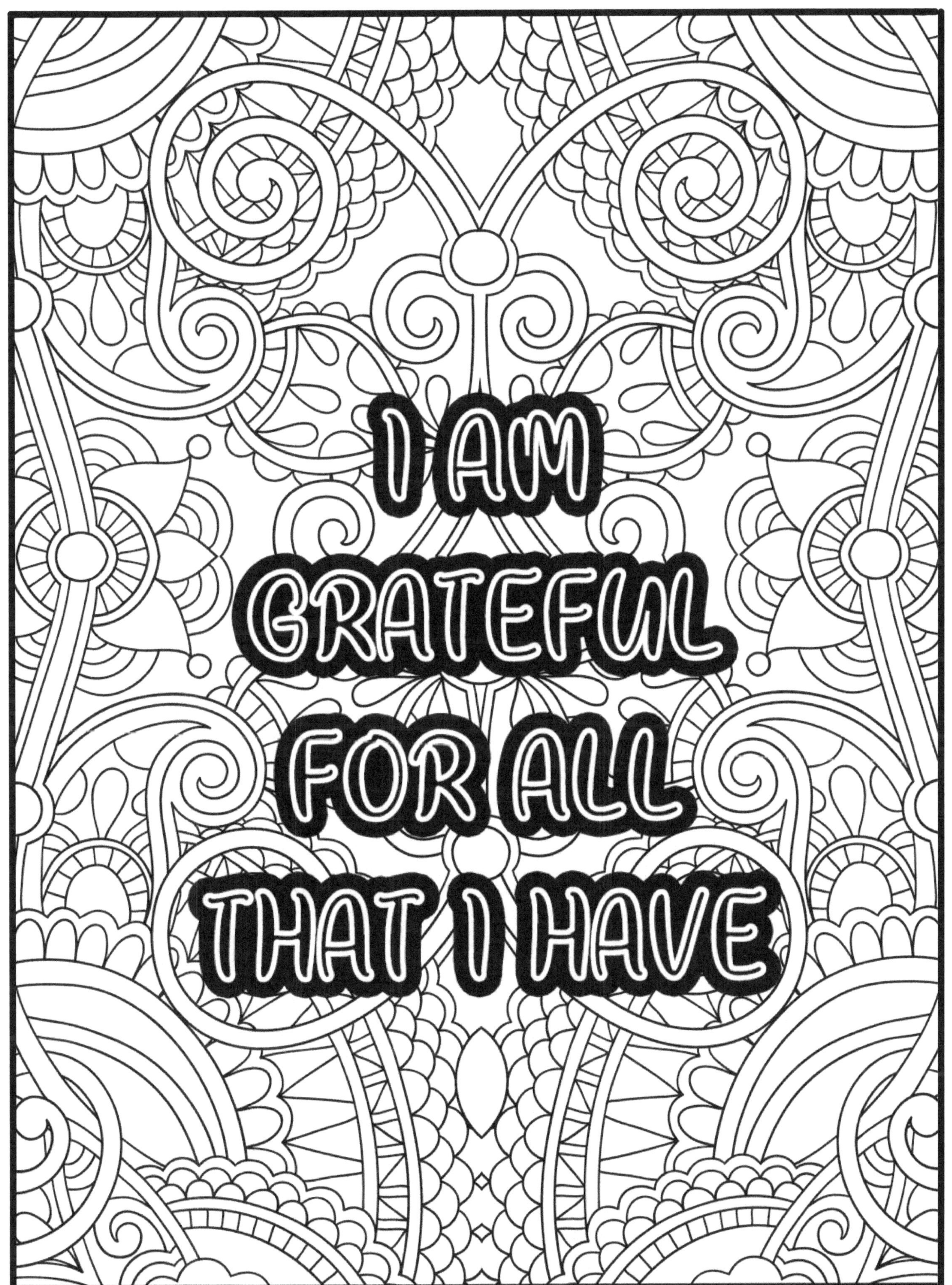
I AM
GRATEFUL
FOR ALL
THAT I HAVE

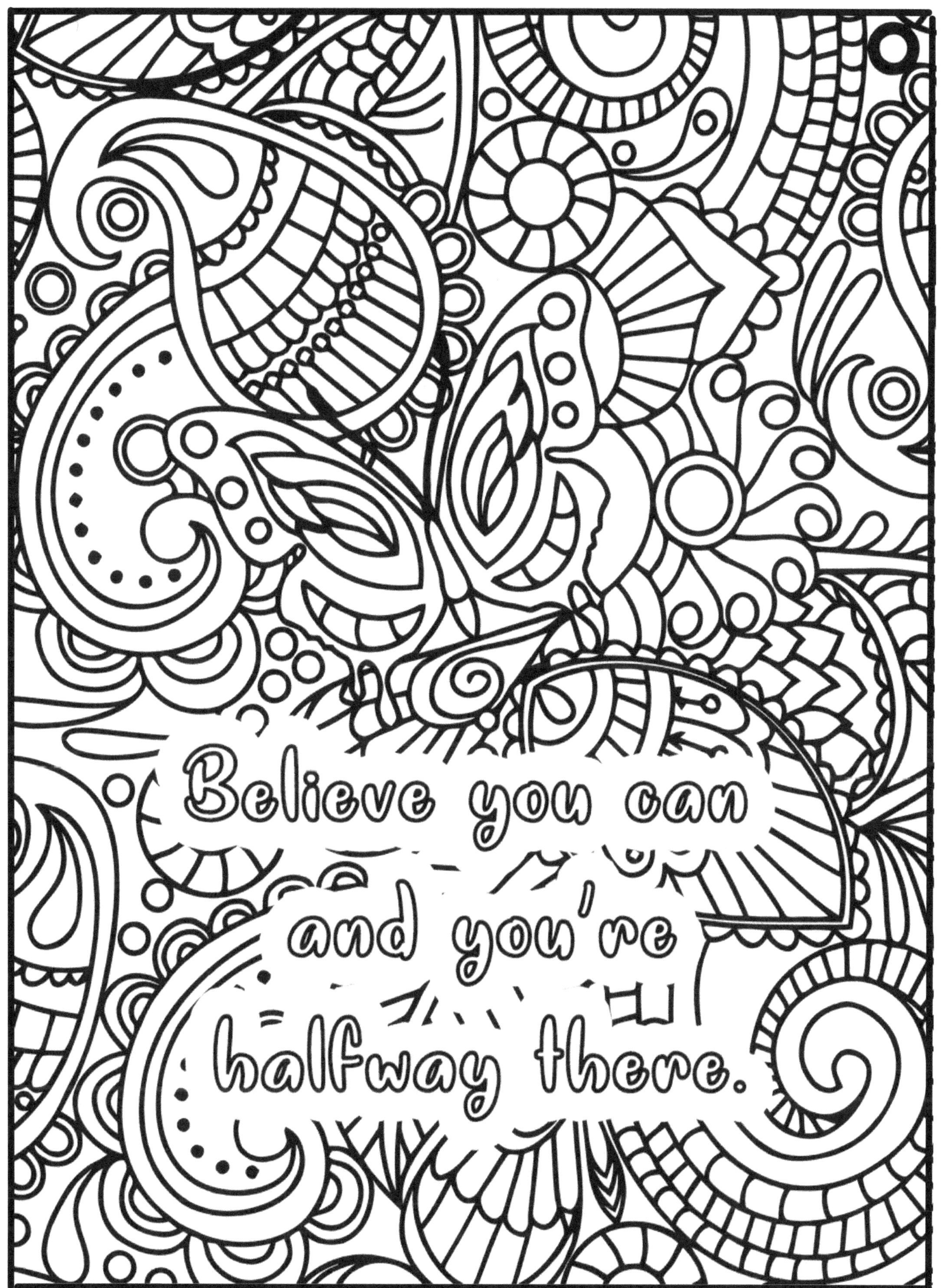

Believe you can
and you're
halfway there.

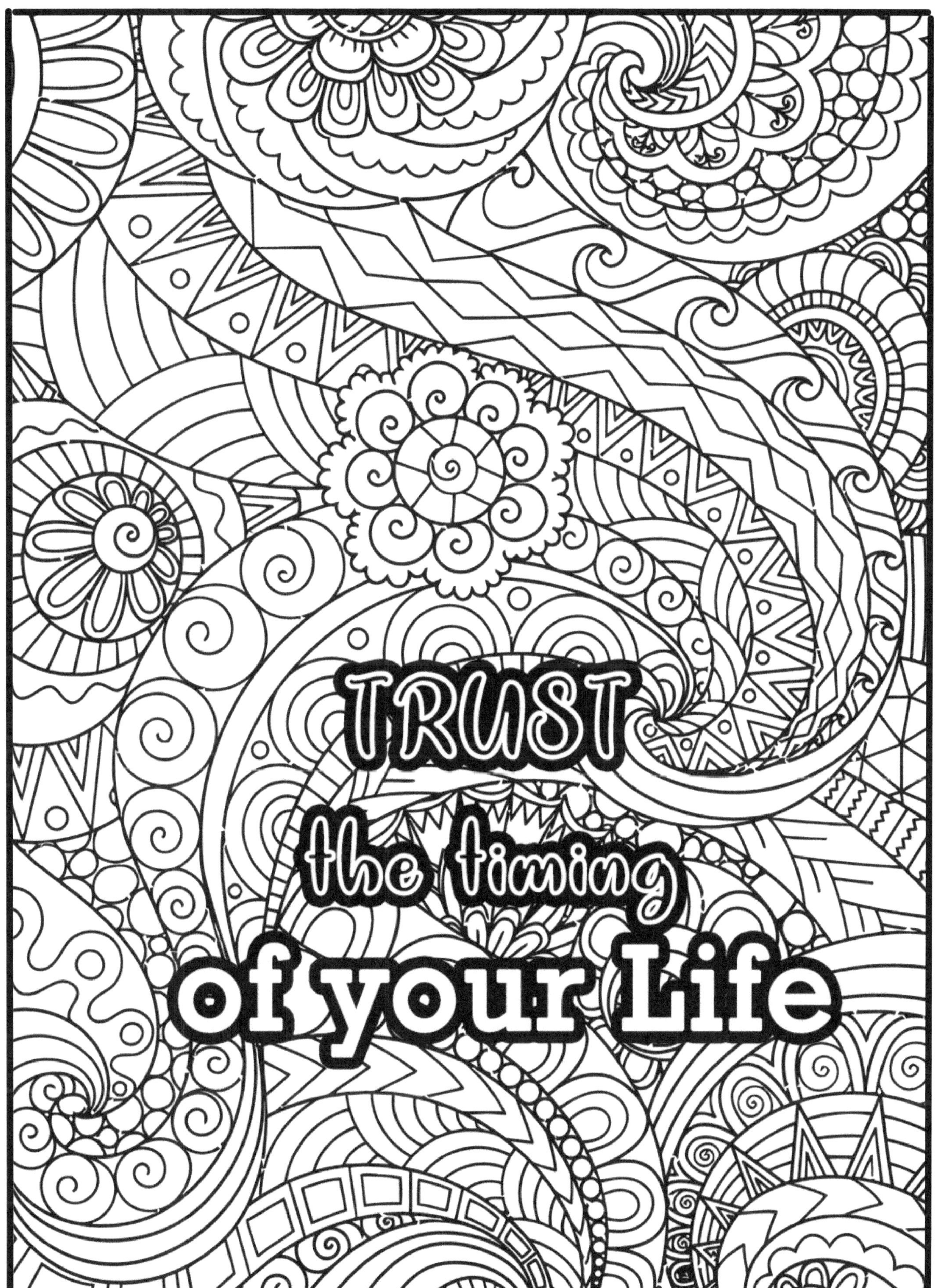

TRUST
the timing
of your Life

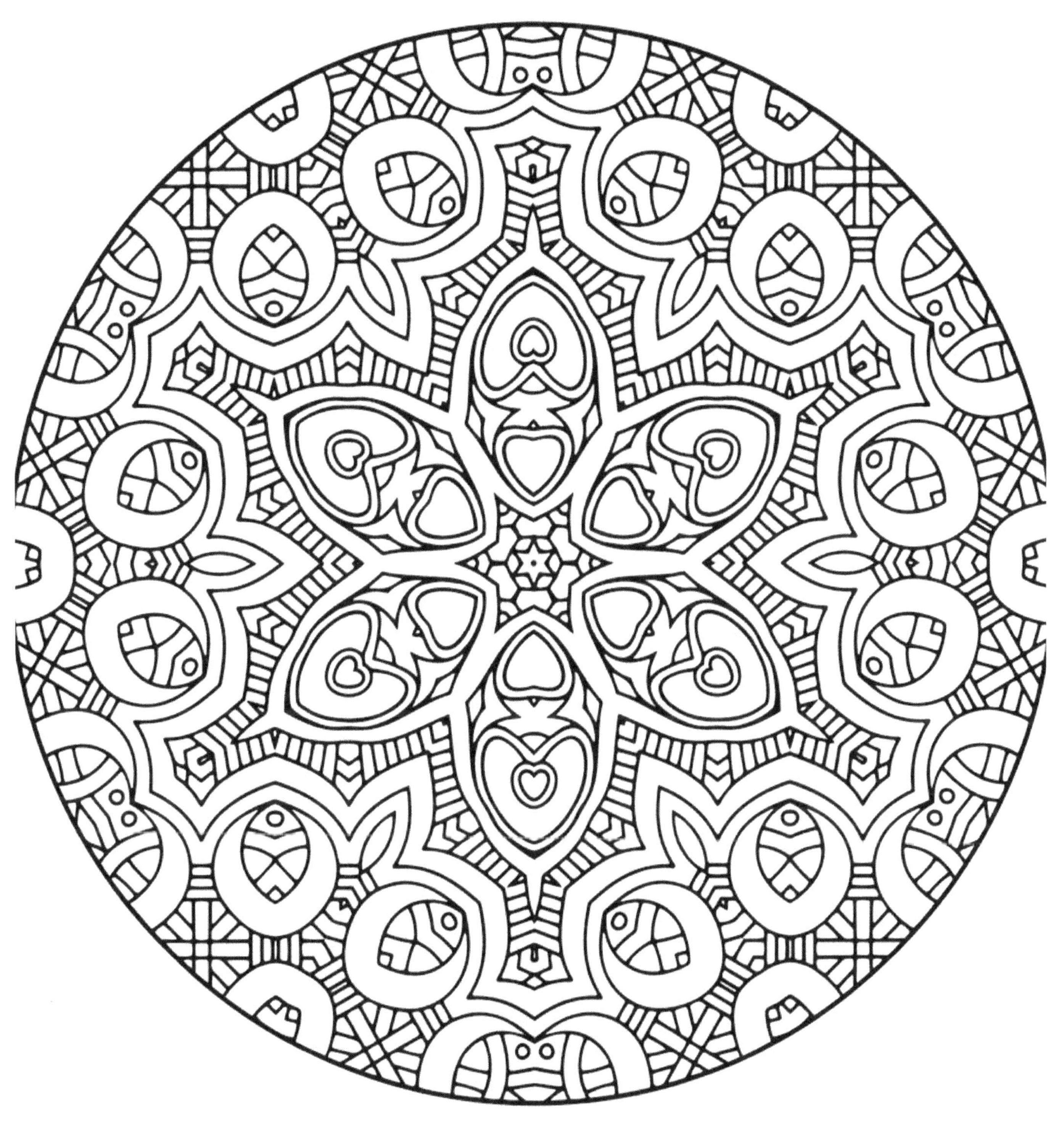

I AM BRAVE, BOLD

and beautiful

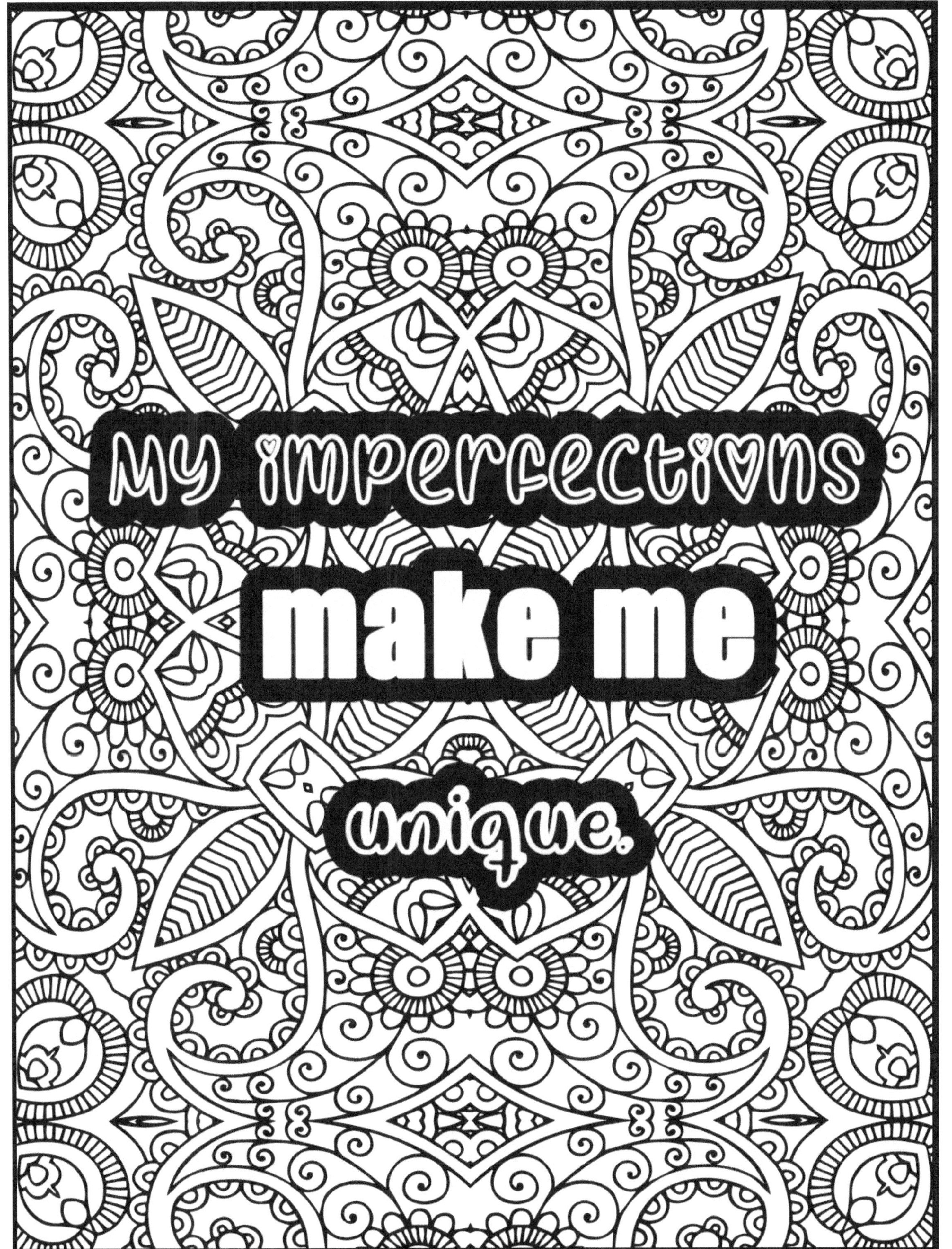

MY imperfections
make me
unique.

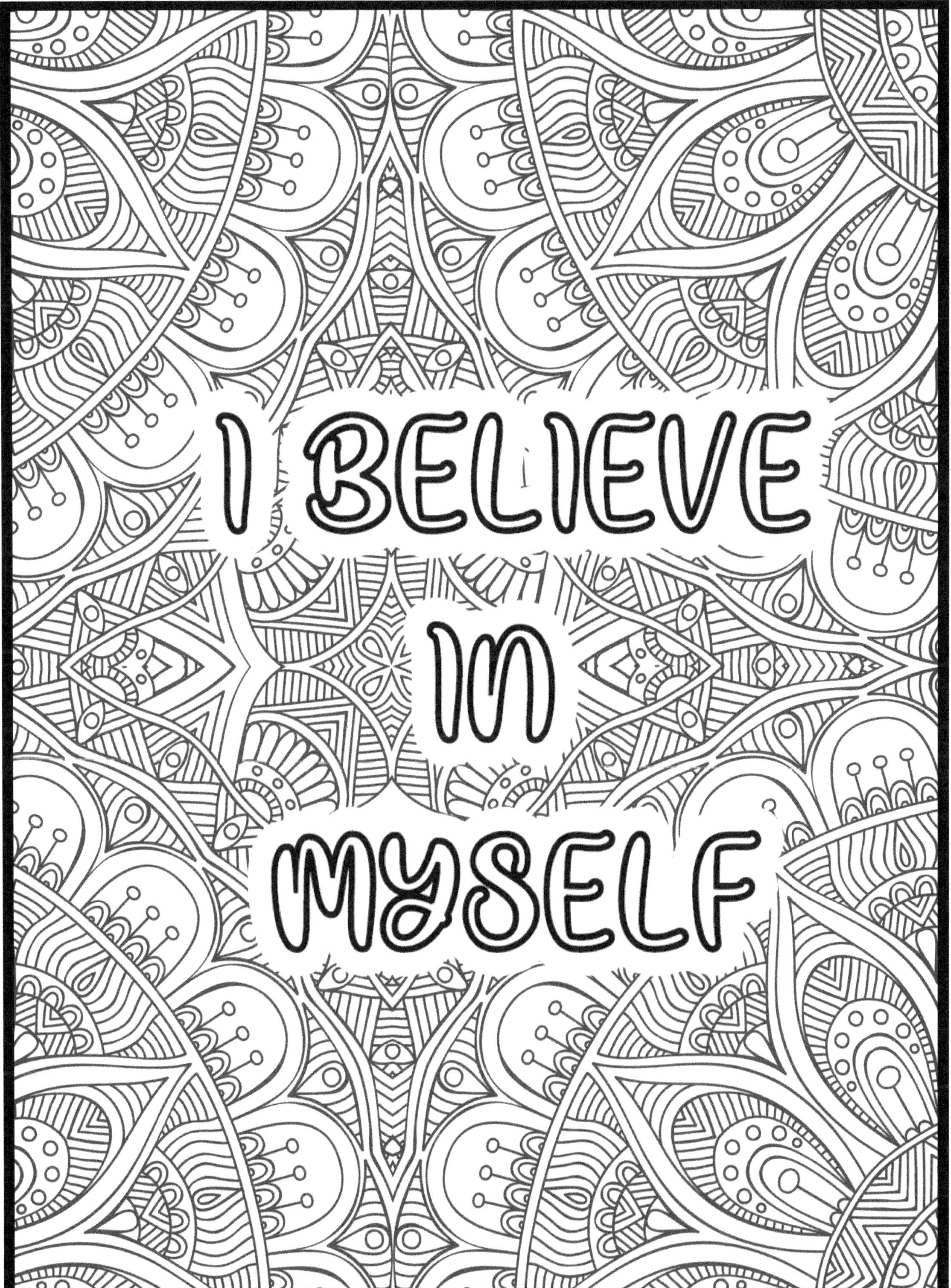

I BELIEVE
IN
MYSELF

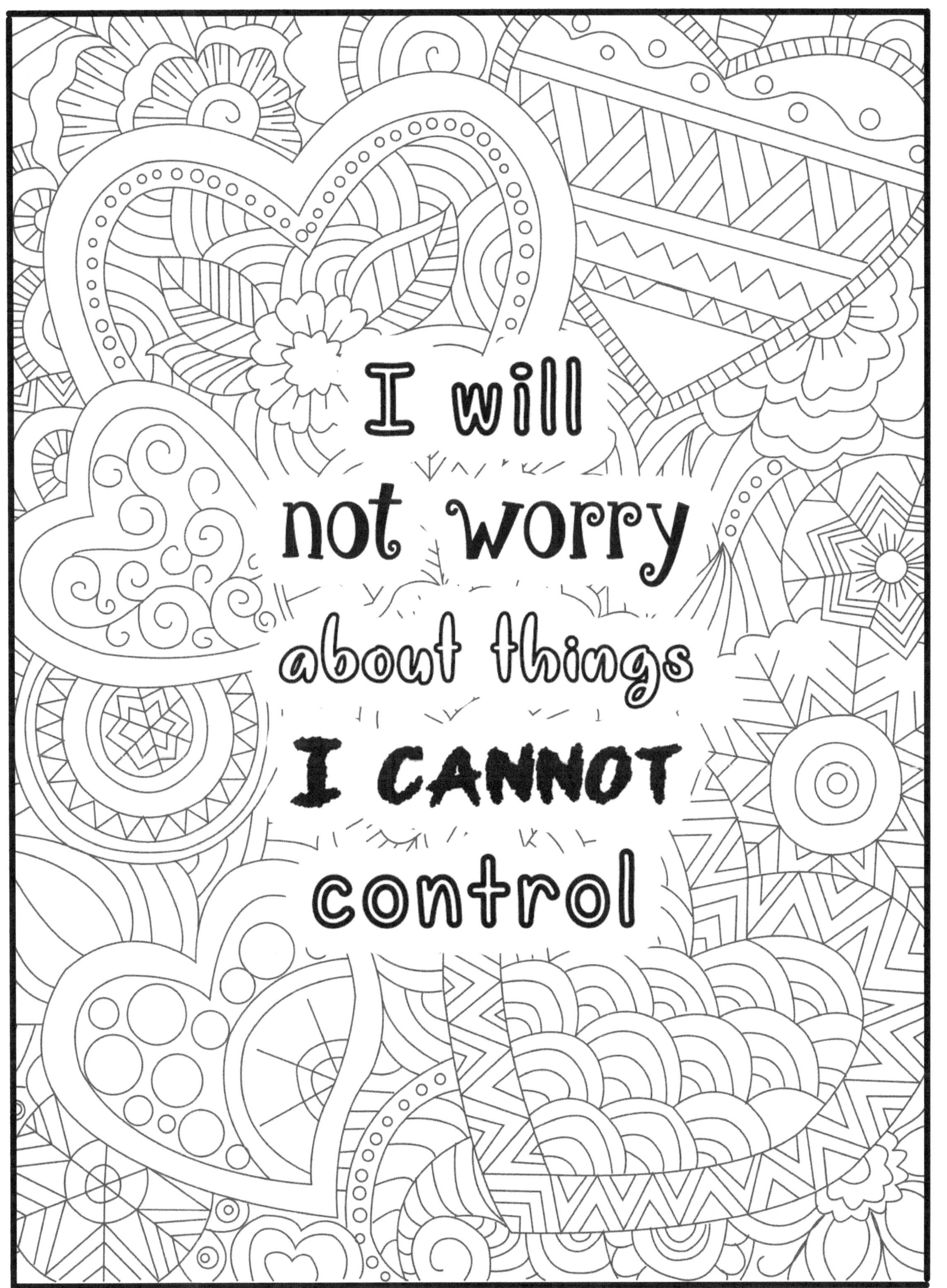

I will
not worry
about things
I CANNOT
control

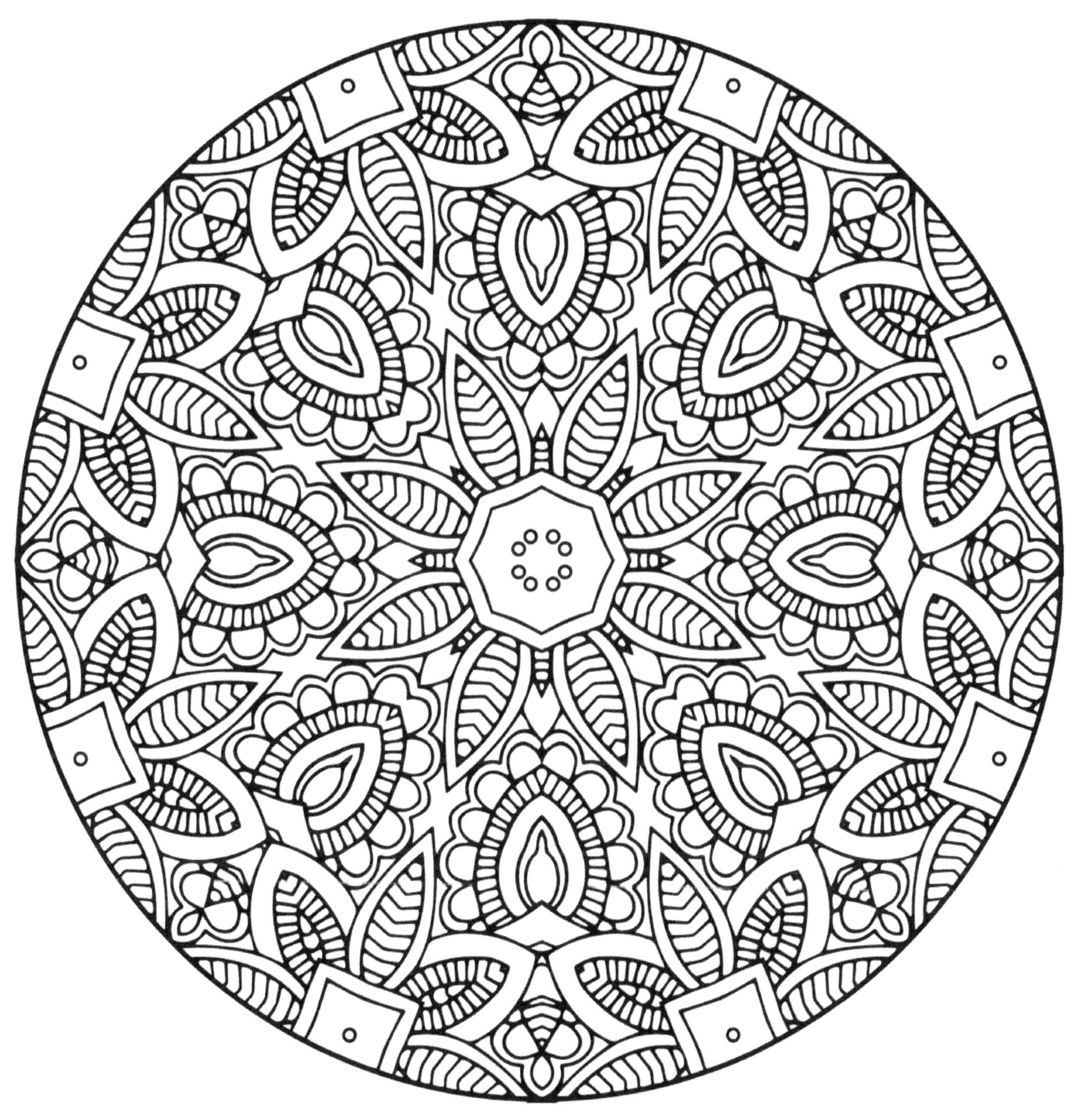

MY CONFIDENCE KNOWS NO LIMITS.

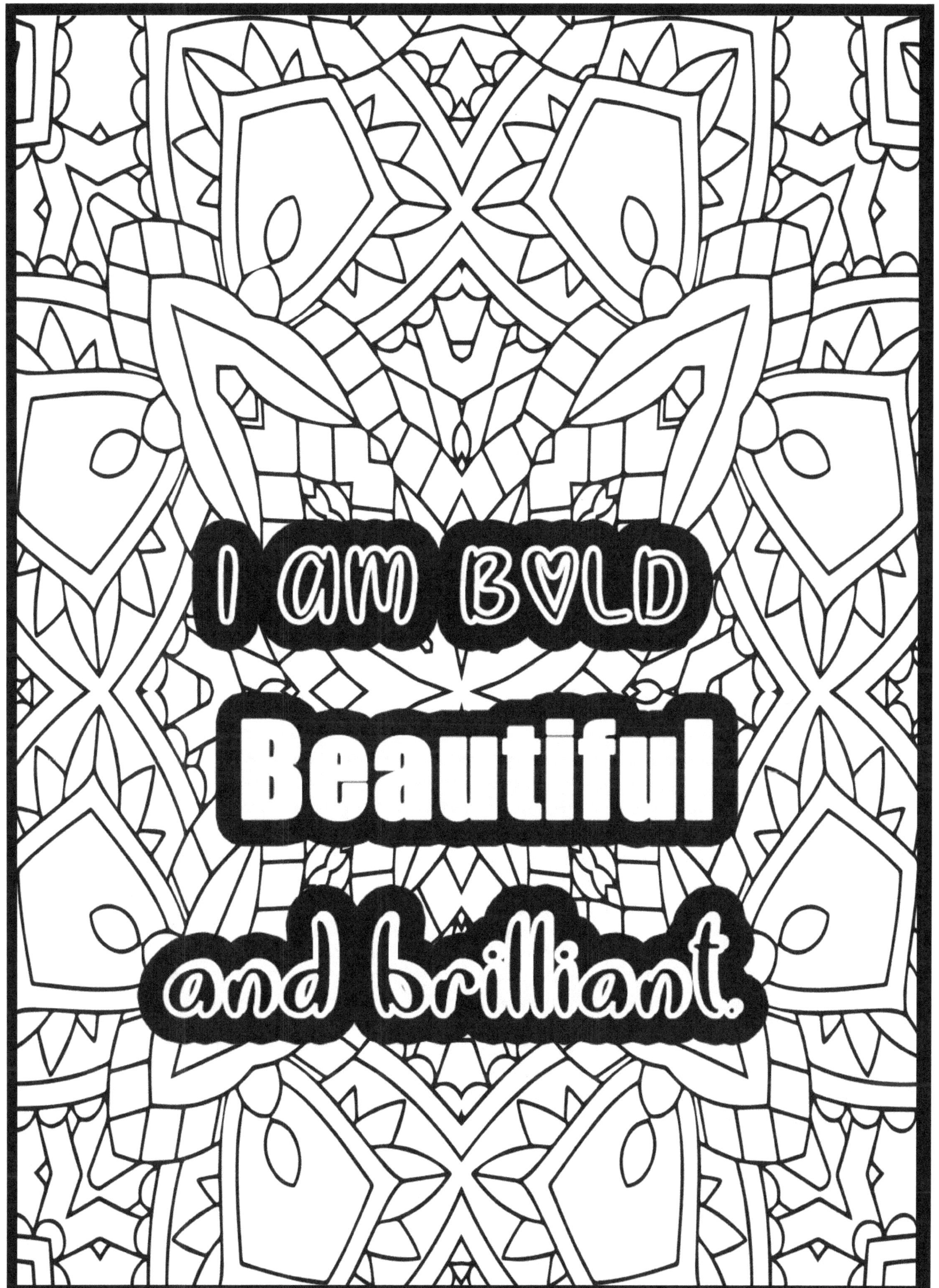

I AM BOLD
Beautiful
and brilliant.

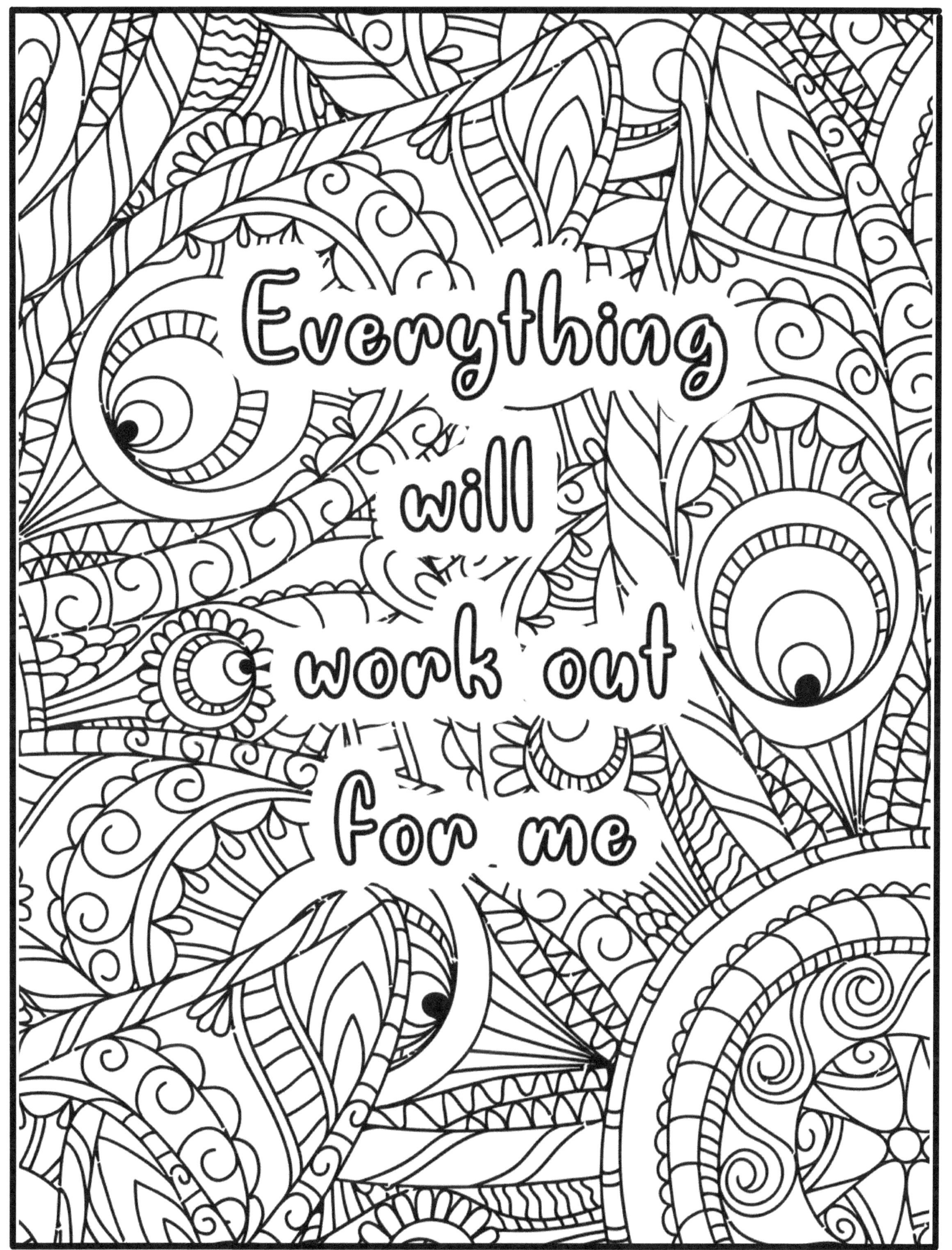

Everything
will
work out
for me

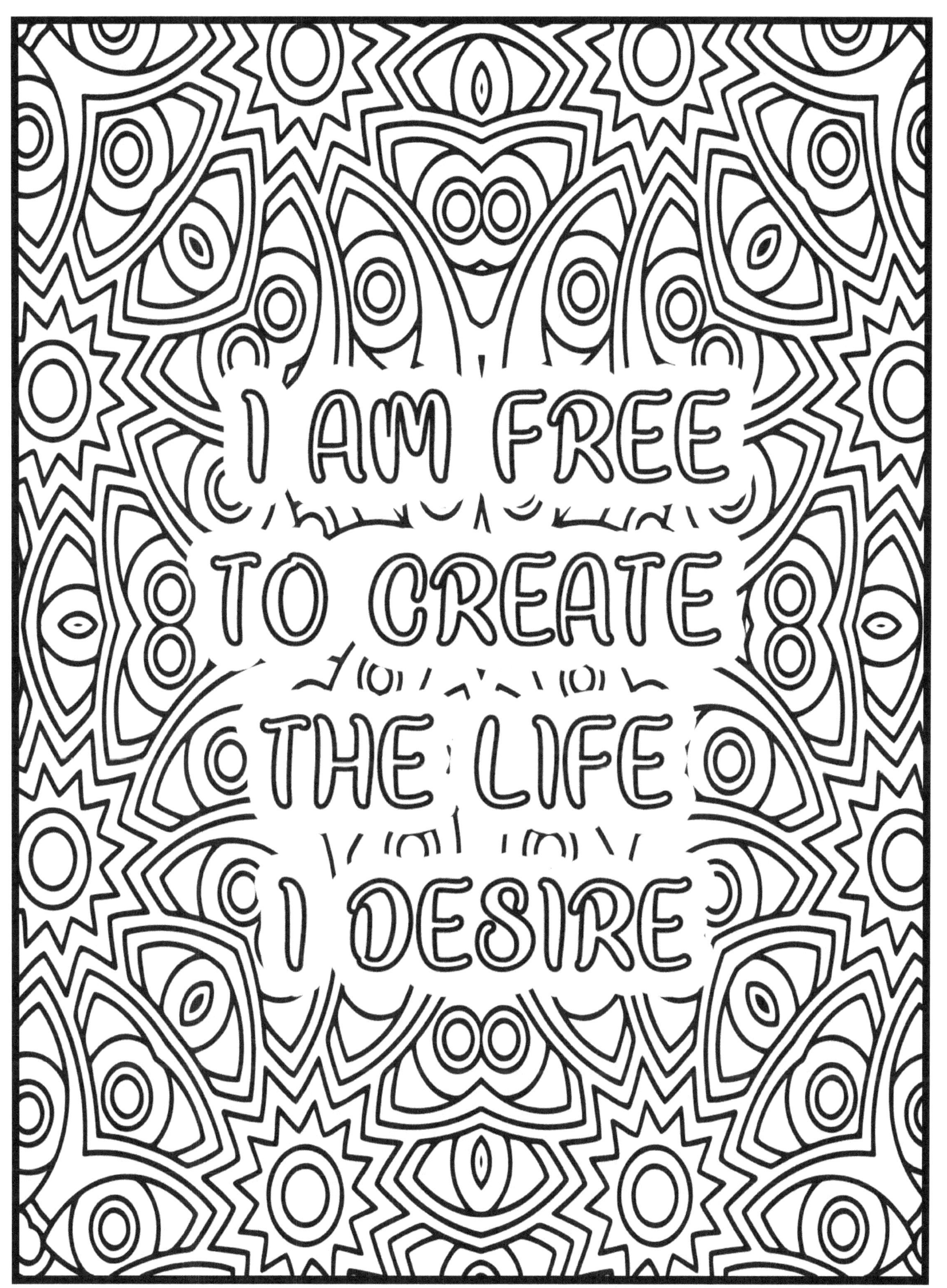

I AM FREE
TO CREATE
THE LIFE
I DESIRE

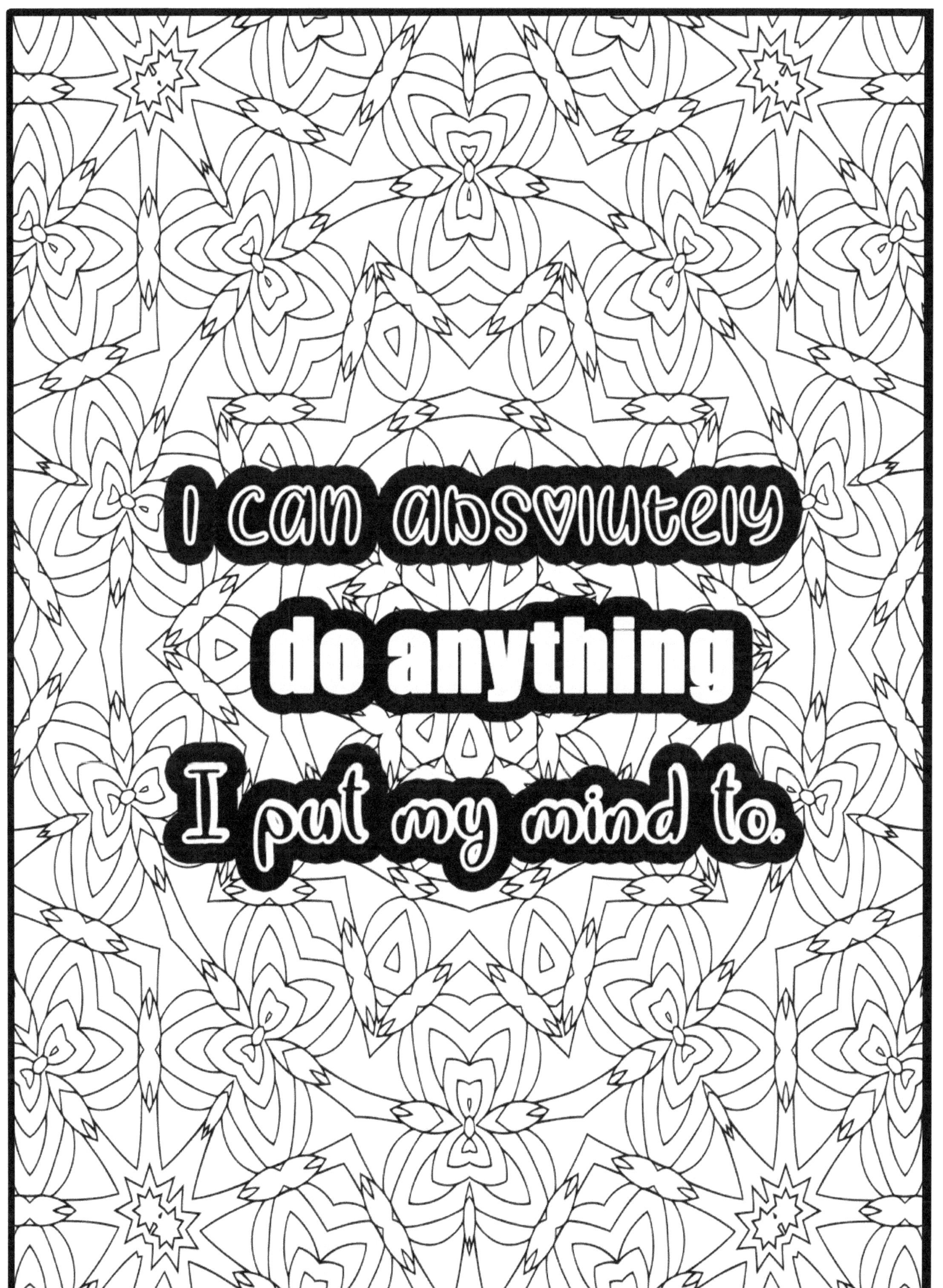

I can absolutely
do anything
I put my mind to.

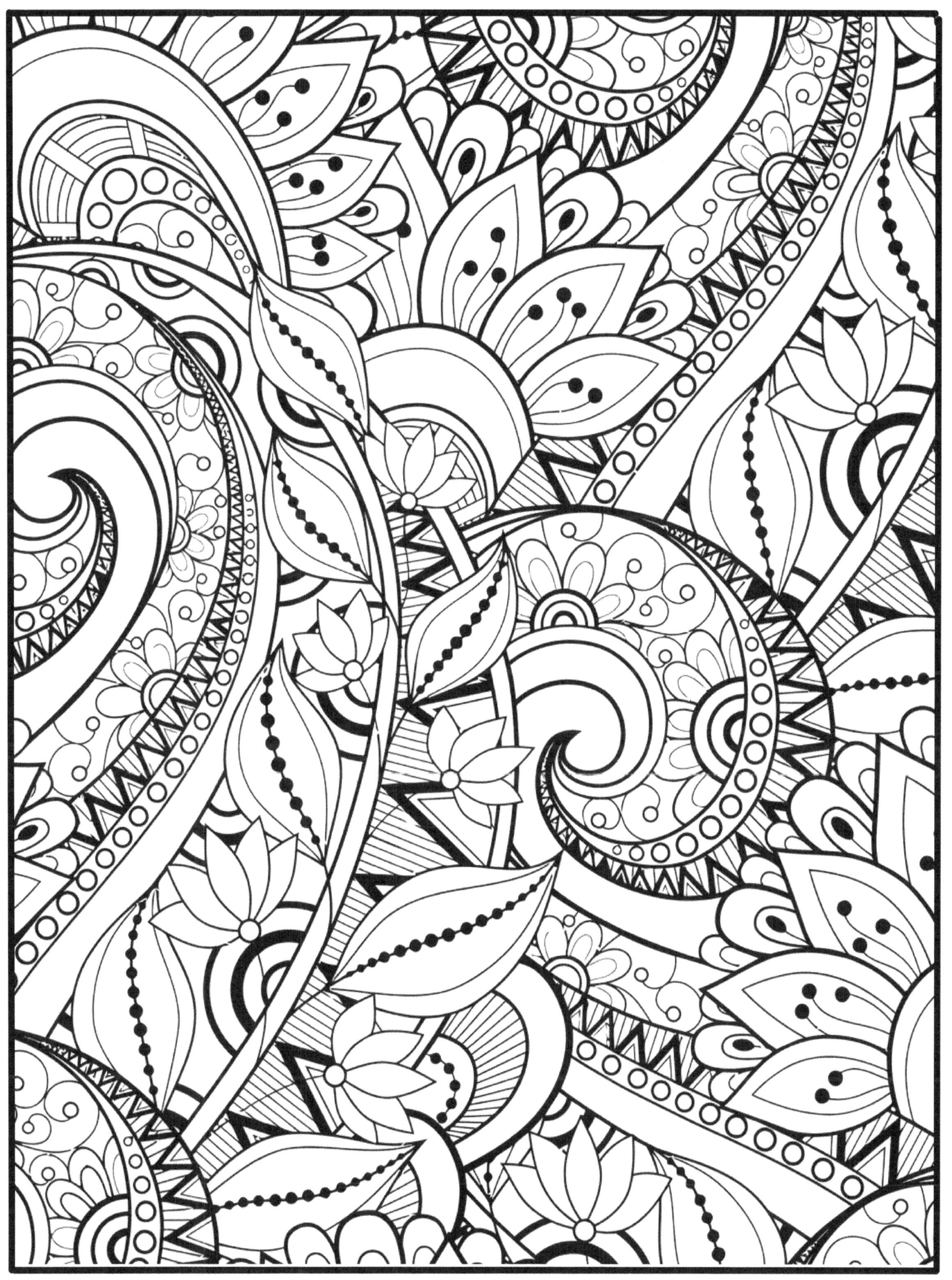

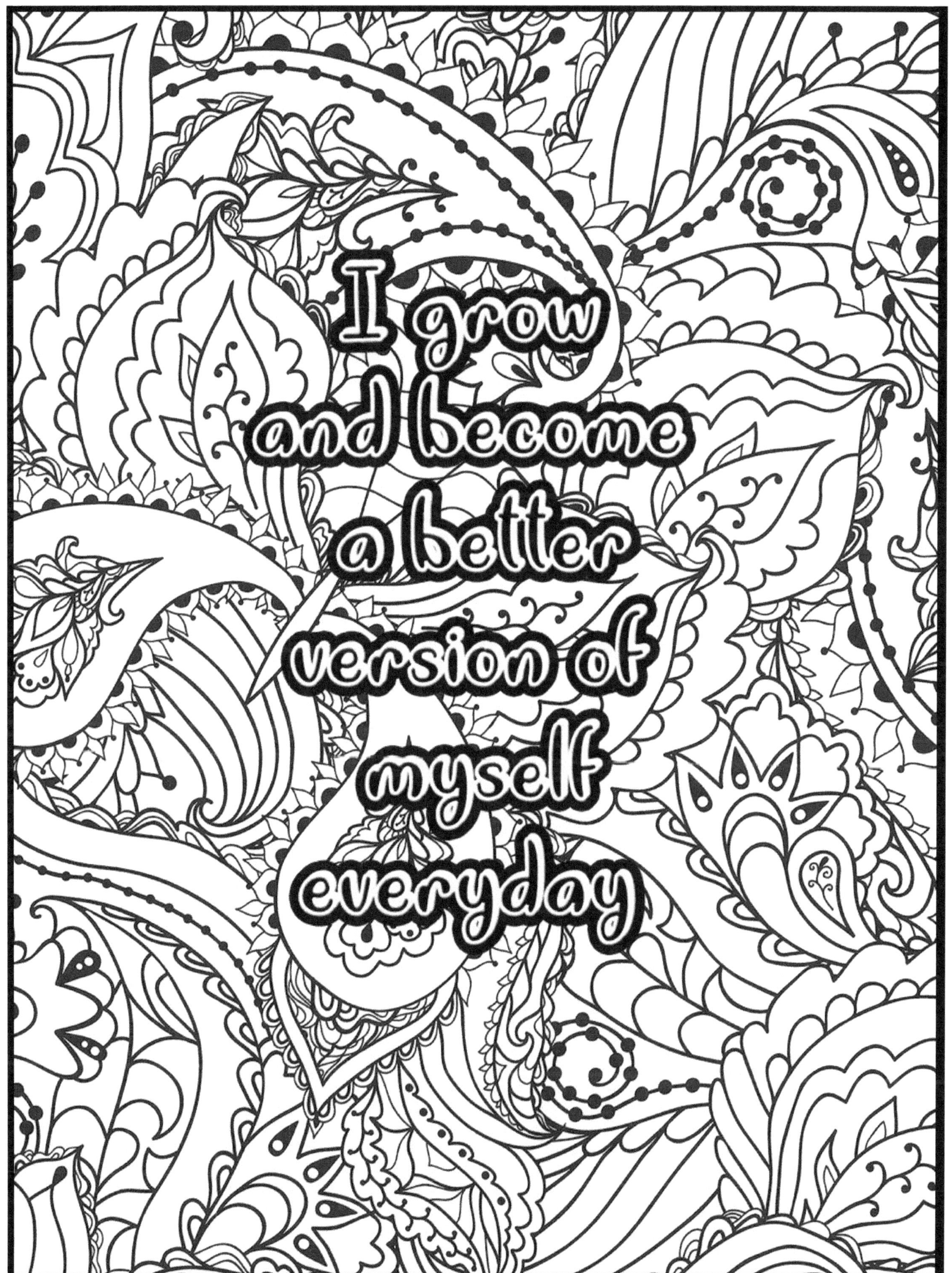

I grow
and become
a better
version of
myself
everyday

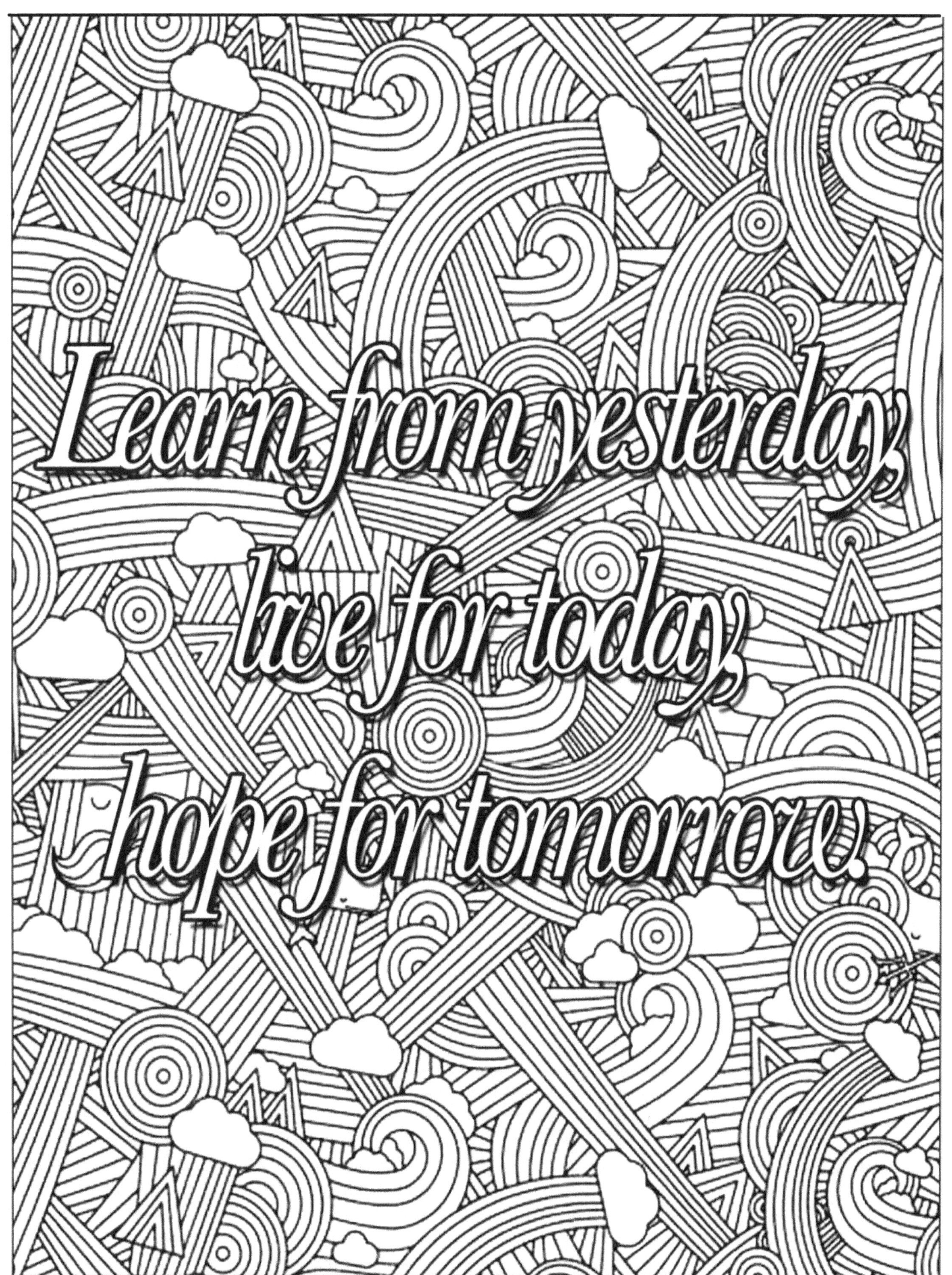

Learn from yesterday,
live for today,
hope for tomorrow.

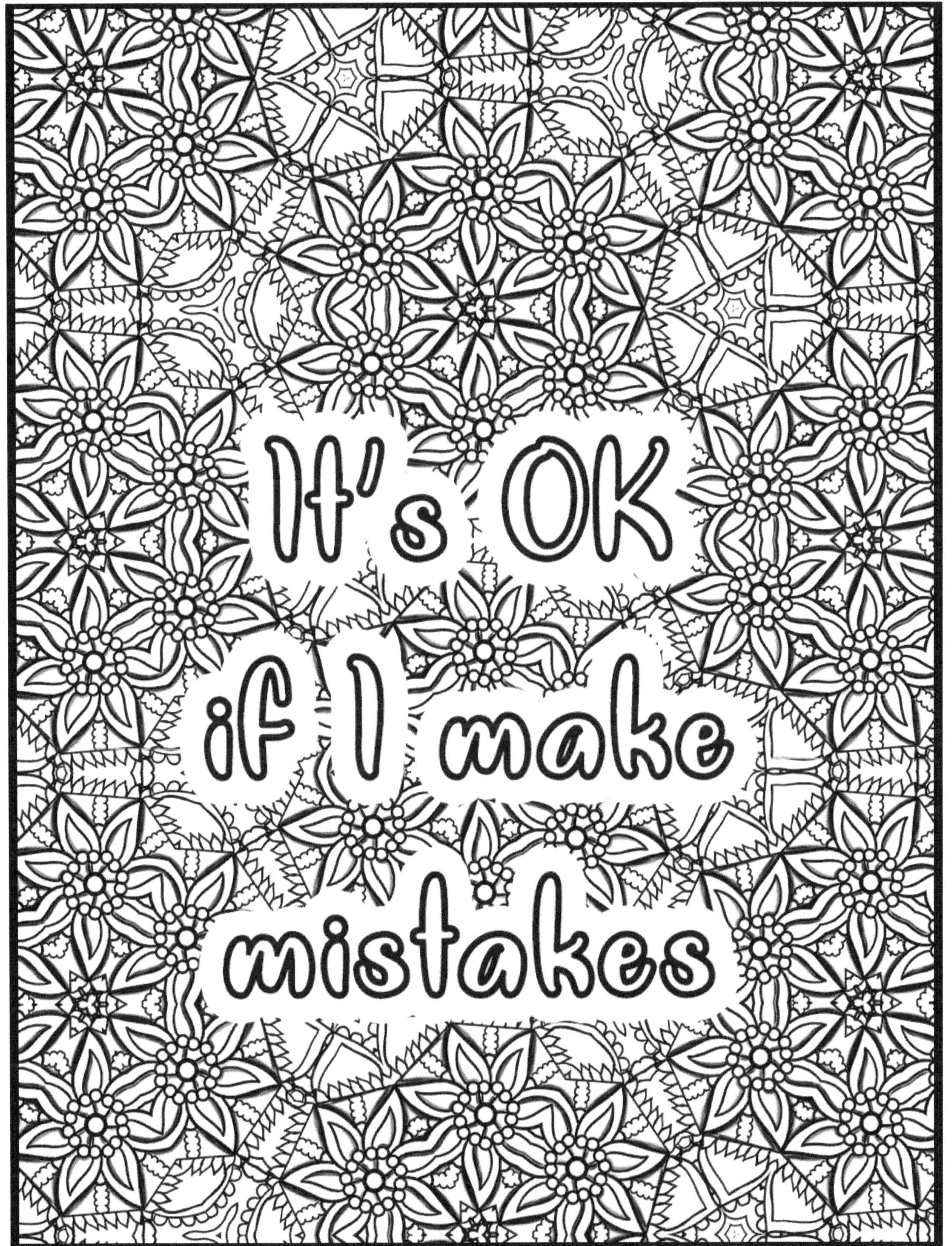

It's OK
if I make
mistakes

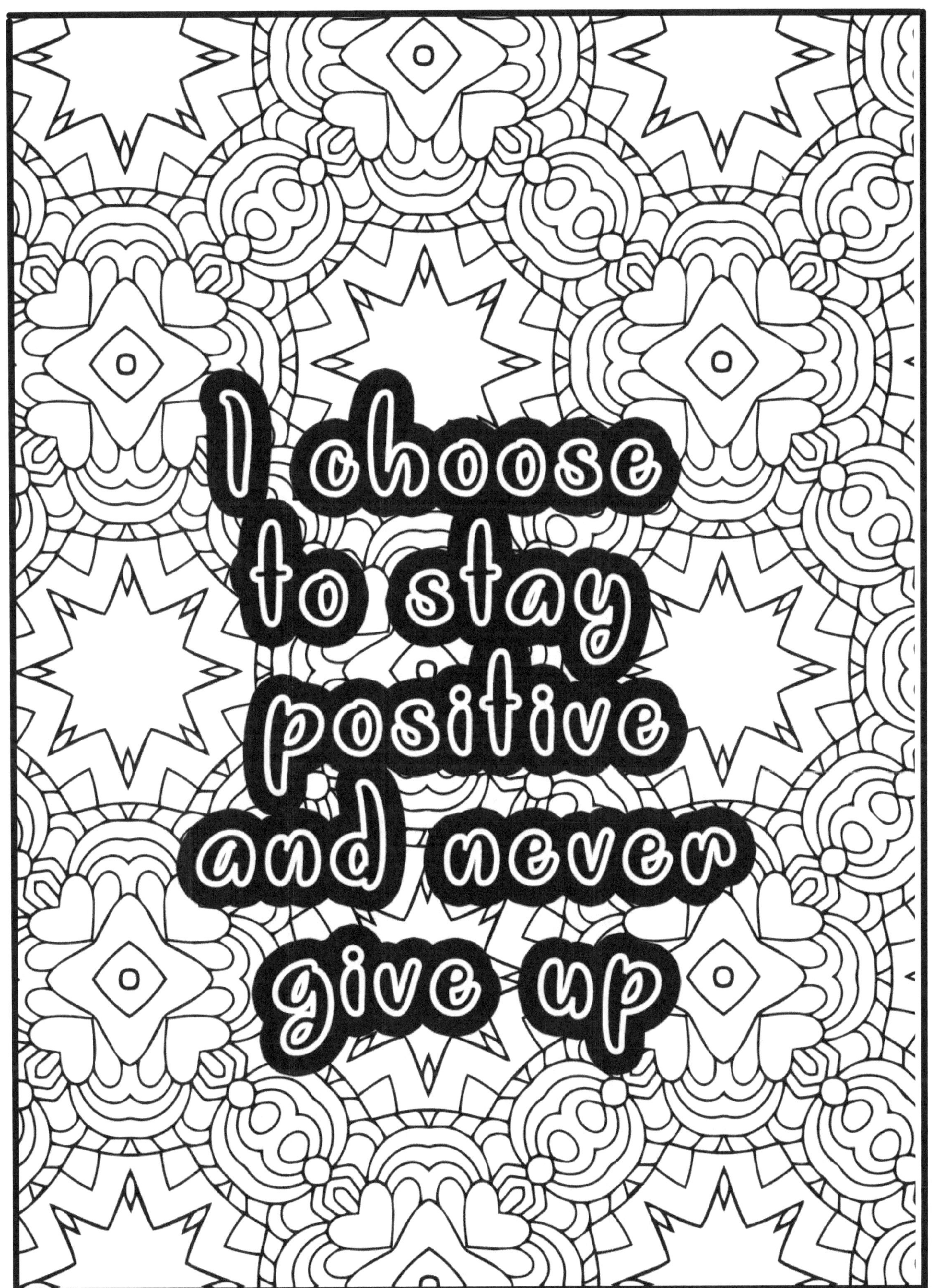

I choose
to stay
positive
and never
give up

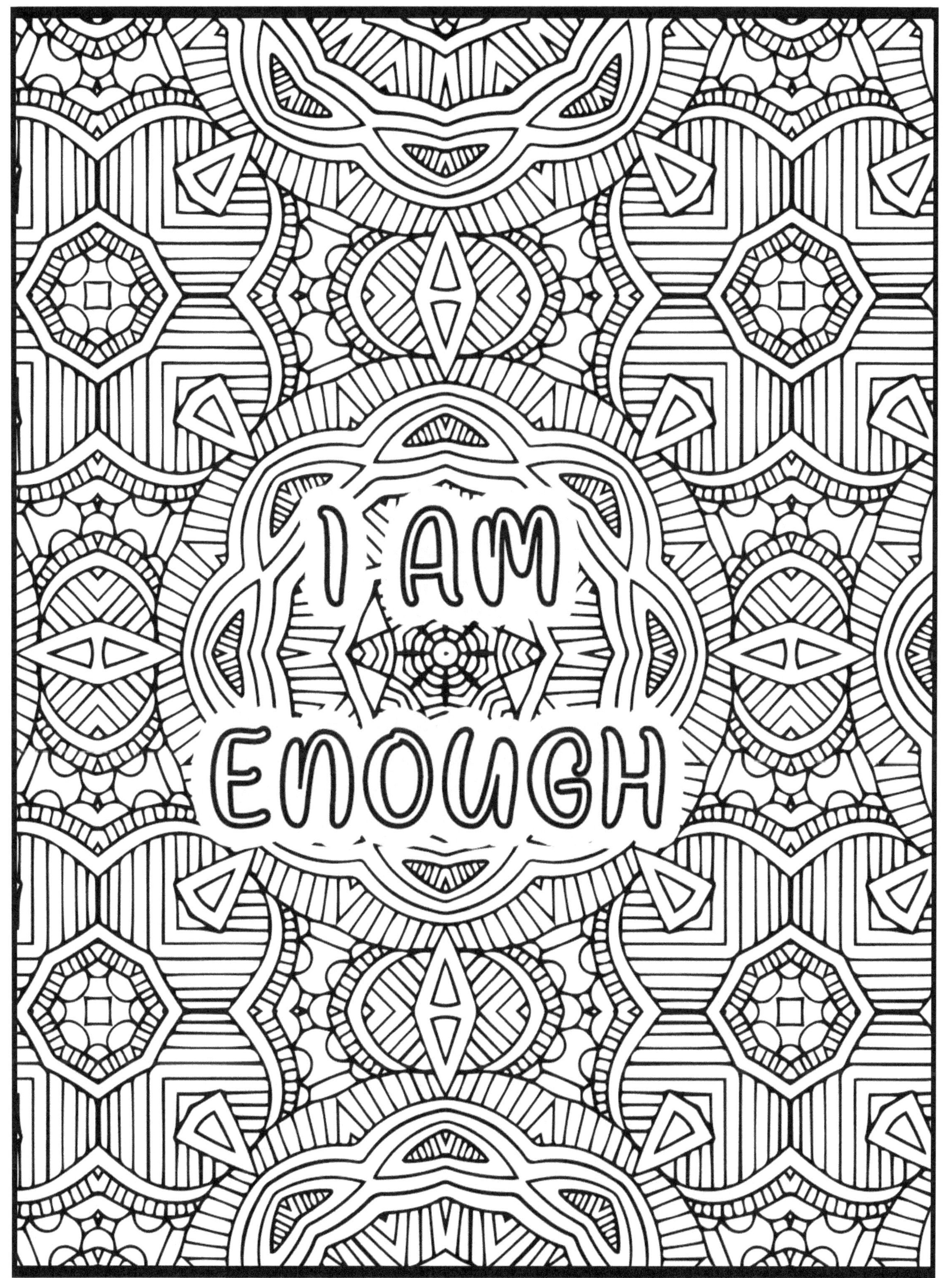

I AM
ENOUGH

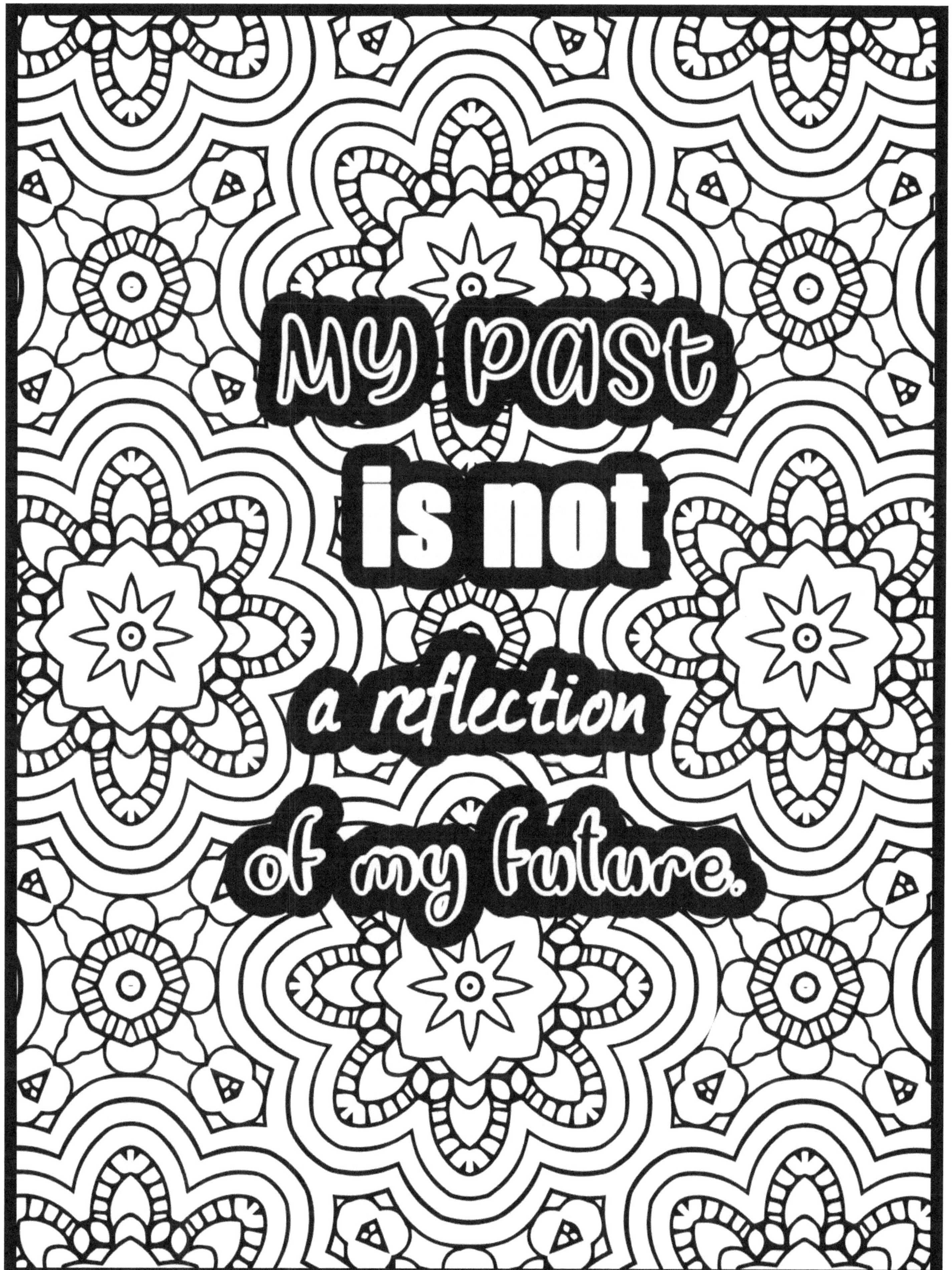

My past
is not
a reflection
of my future.

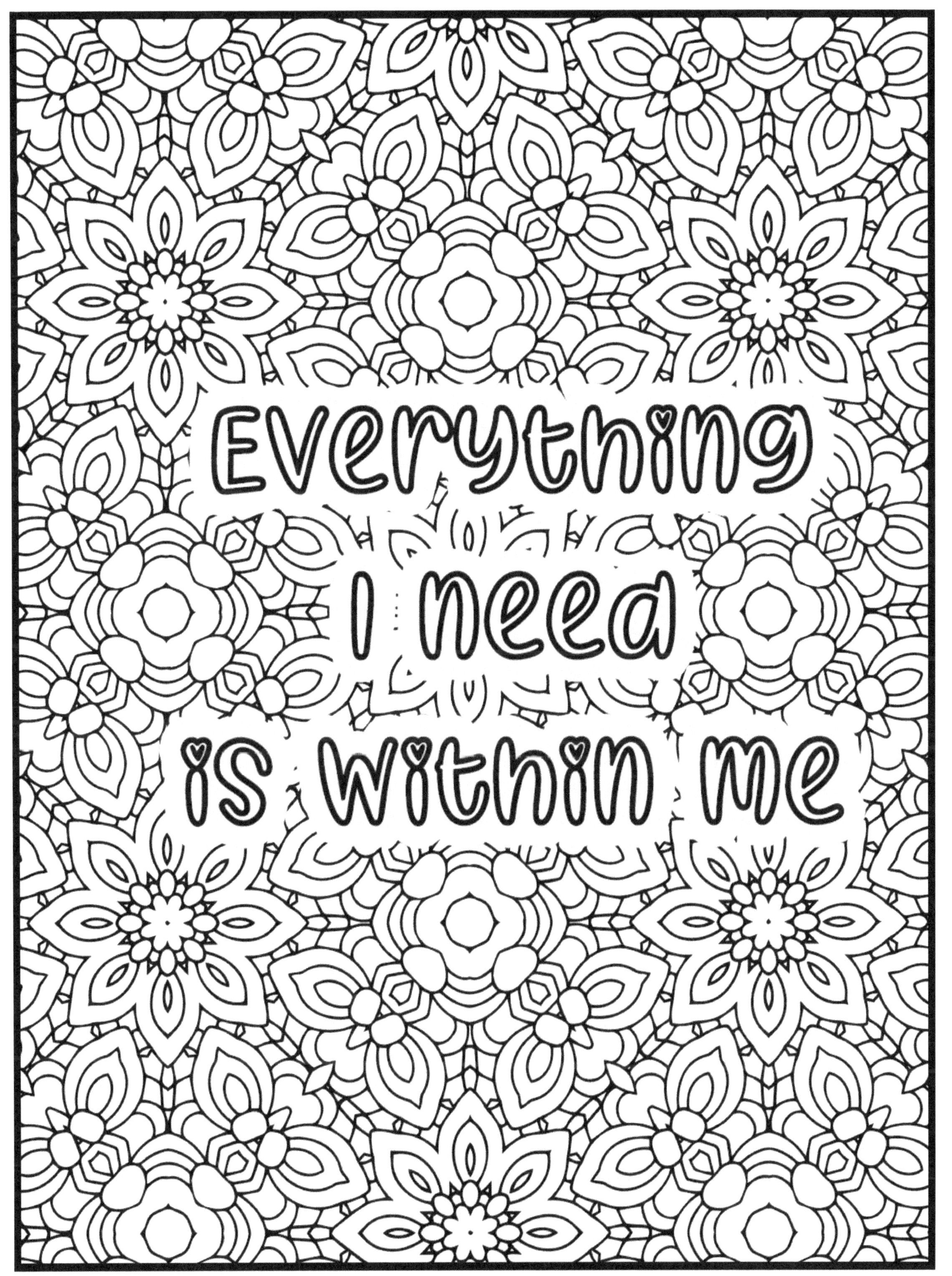

Everything
I need
is within me

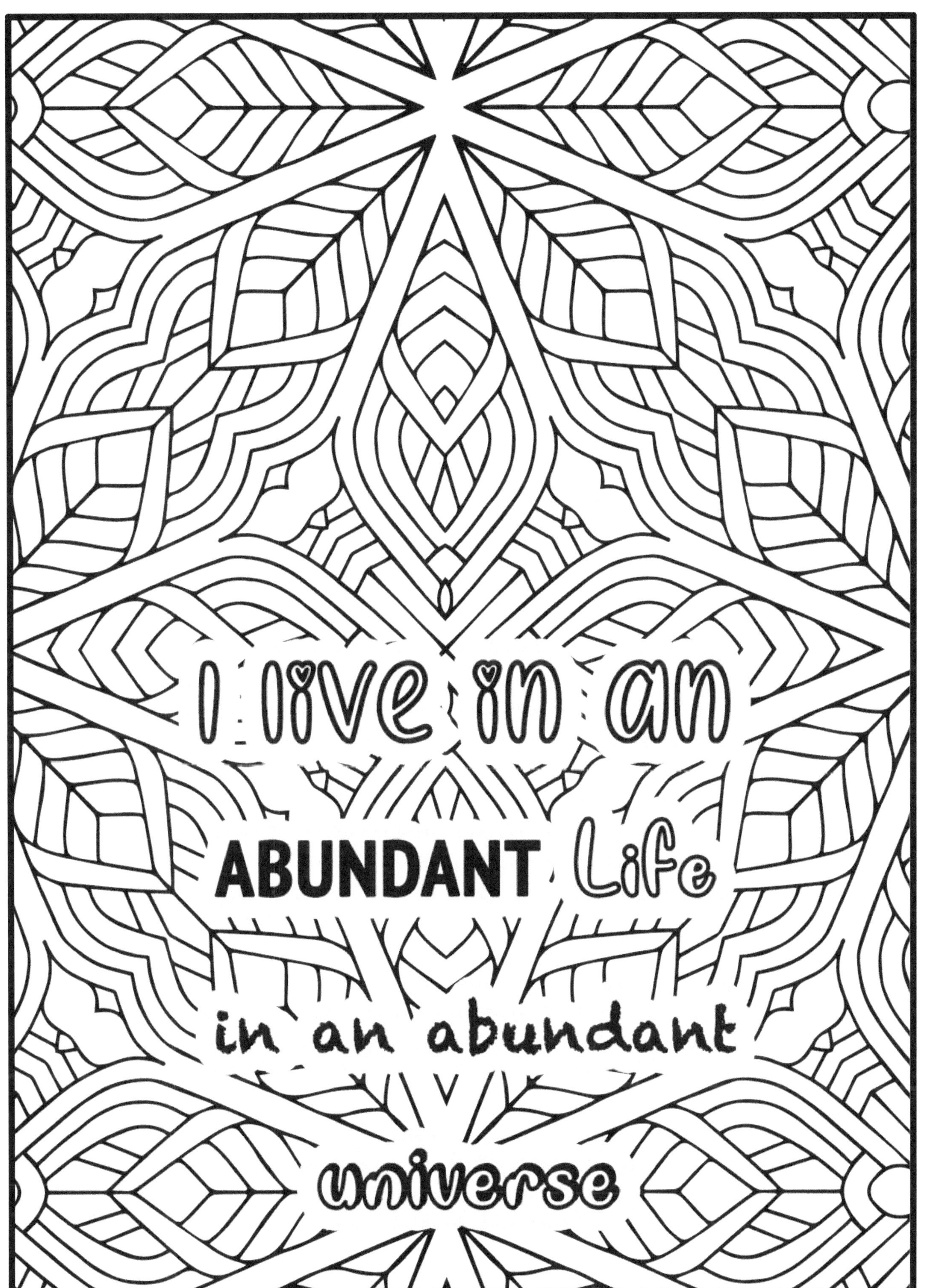

I live in an
ABUNDANT Life
in an abundant
universe

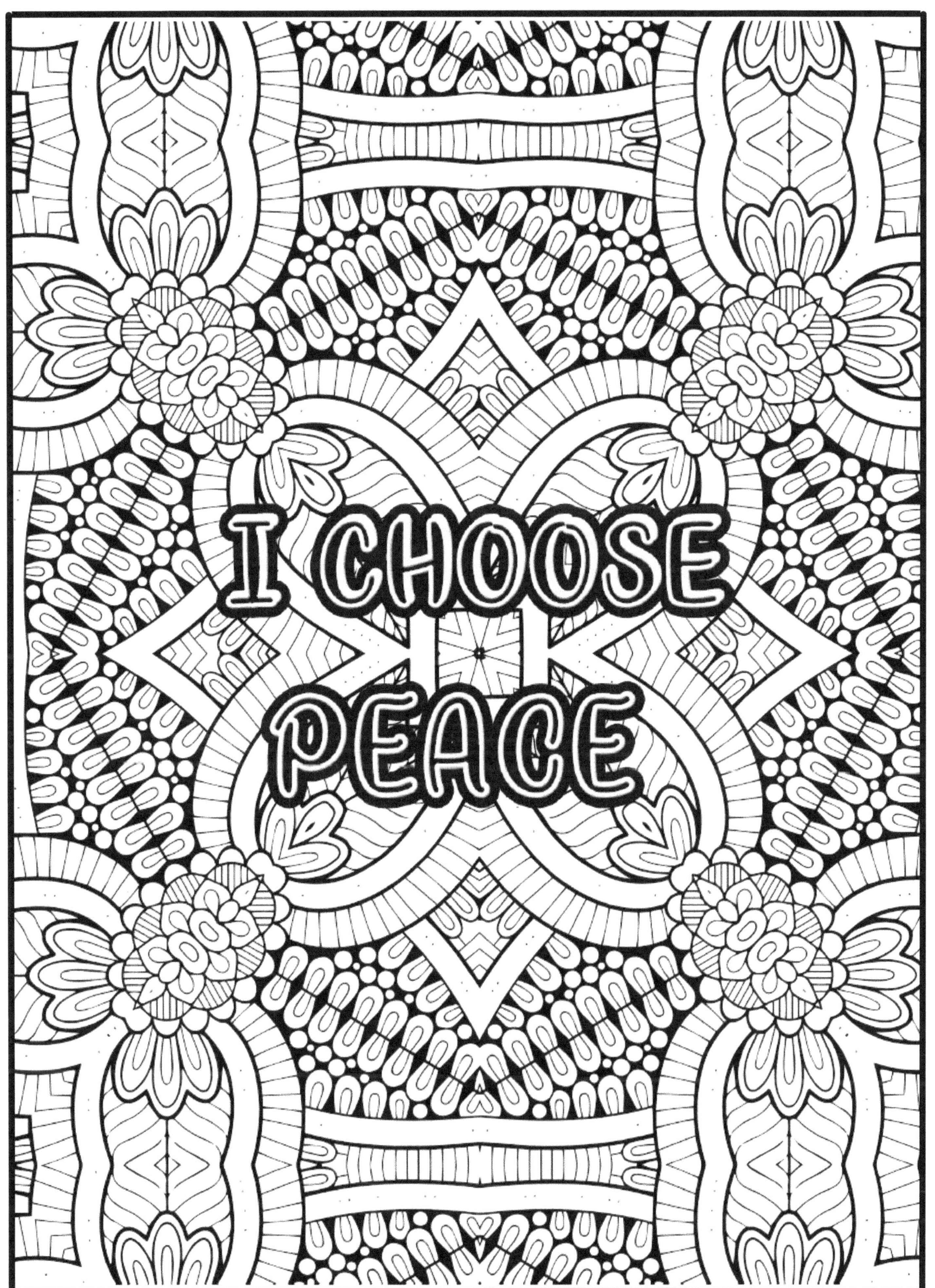
I CHOOSE
PEACE

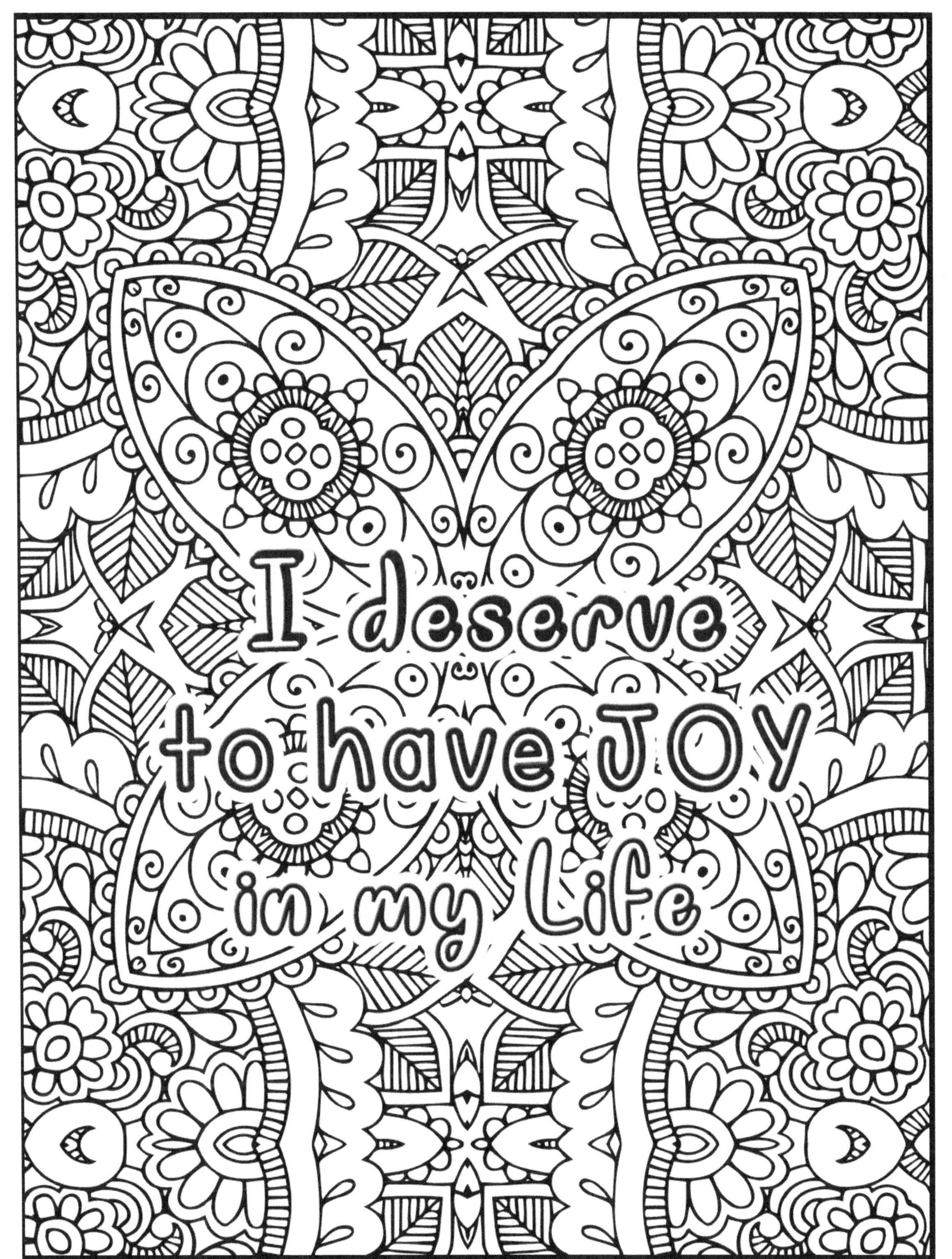

I deserve
to have JOY
in my Life

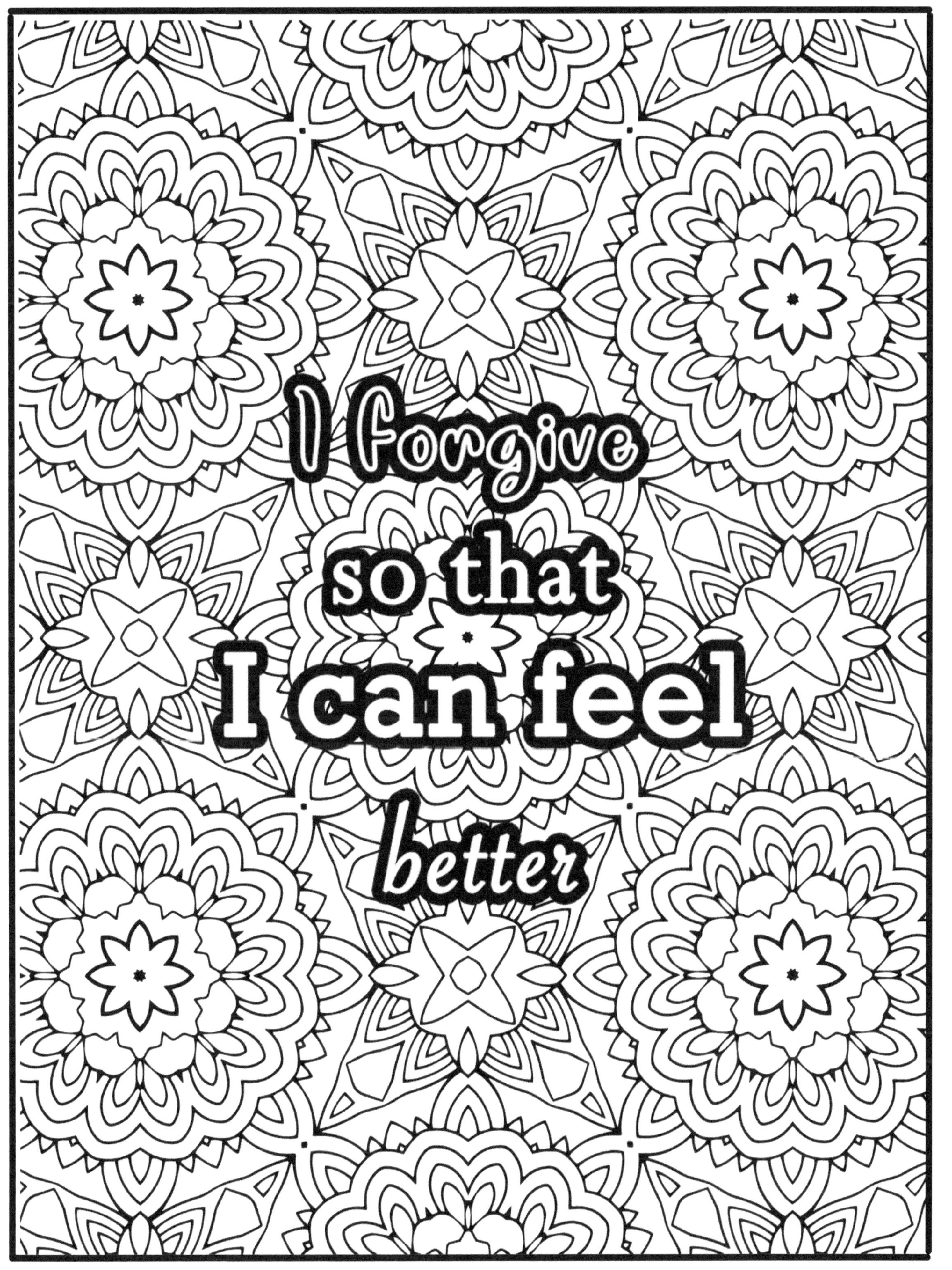

I forgive
so that
I can feel
better

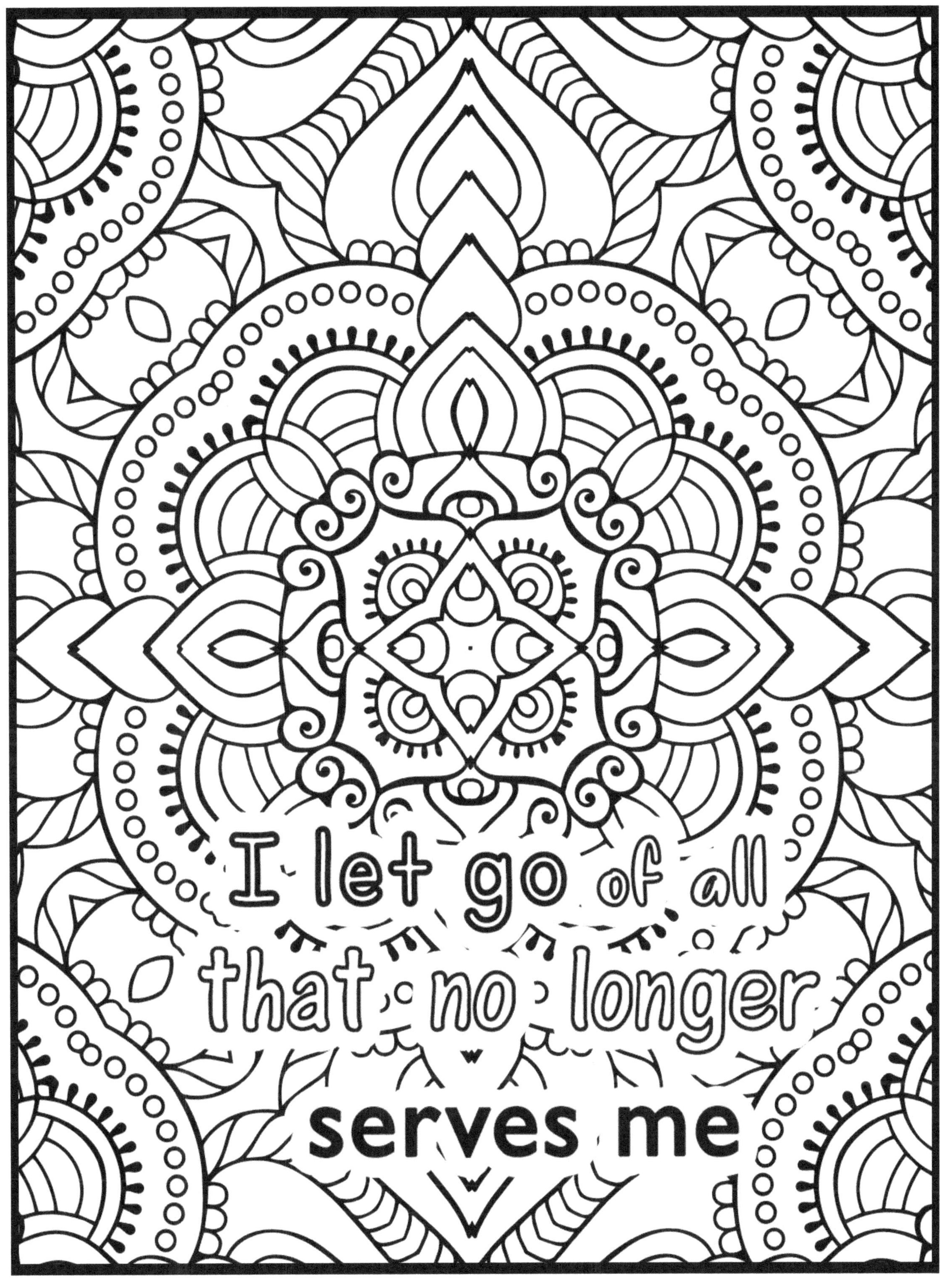

I let go of all
that no longer
serves me

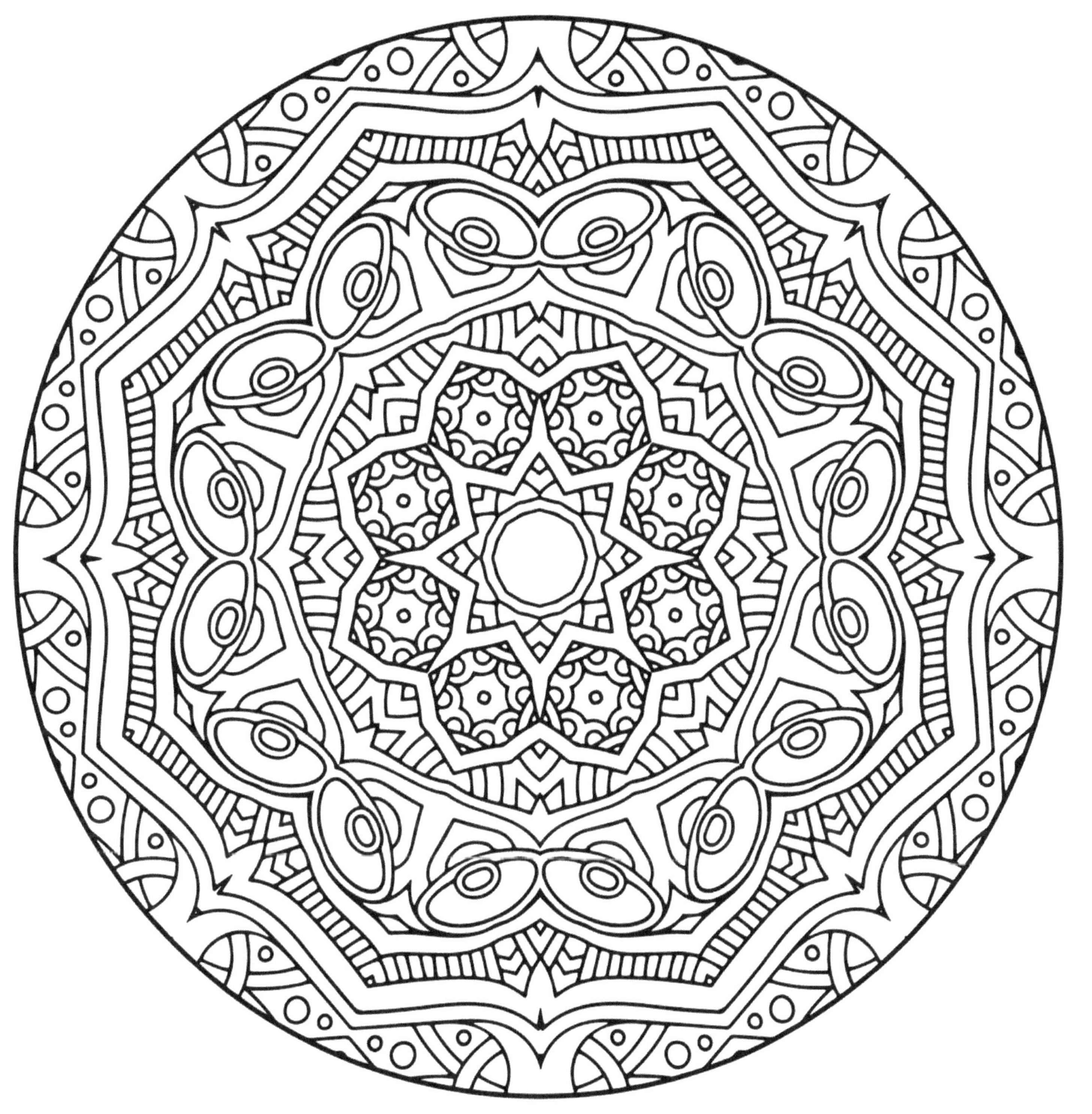

I accept myself
unconditionally

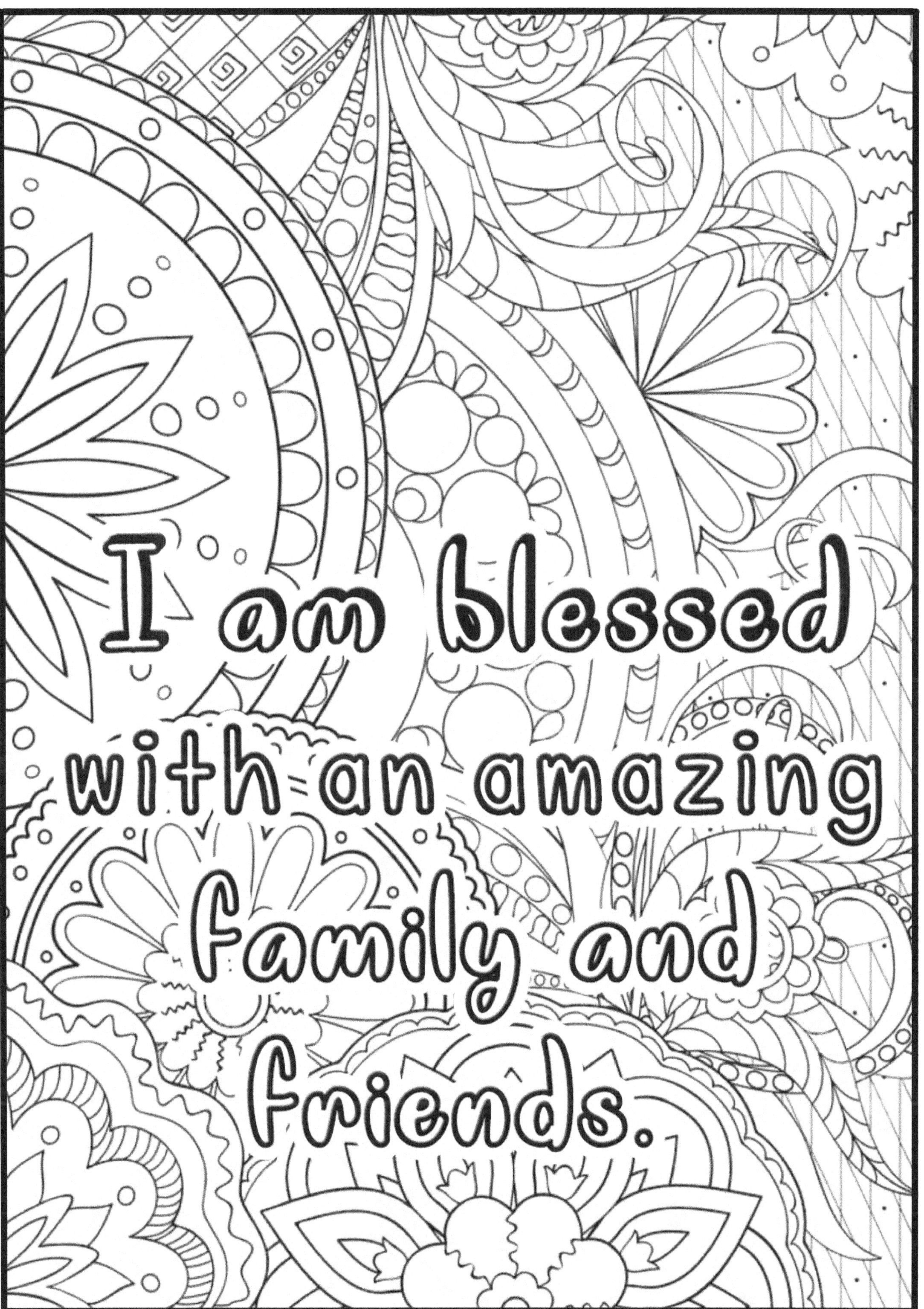

I am blessed
with an amazing
family and
friends.

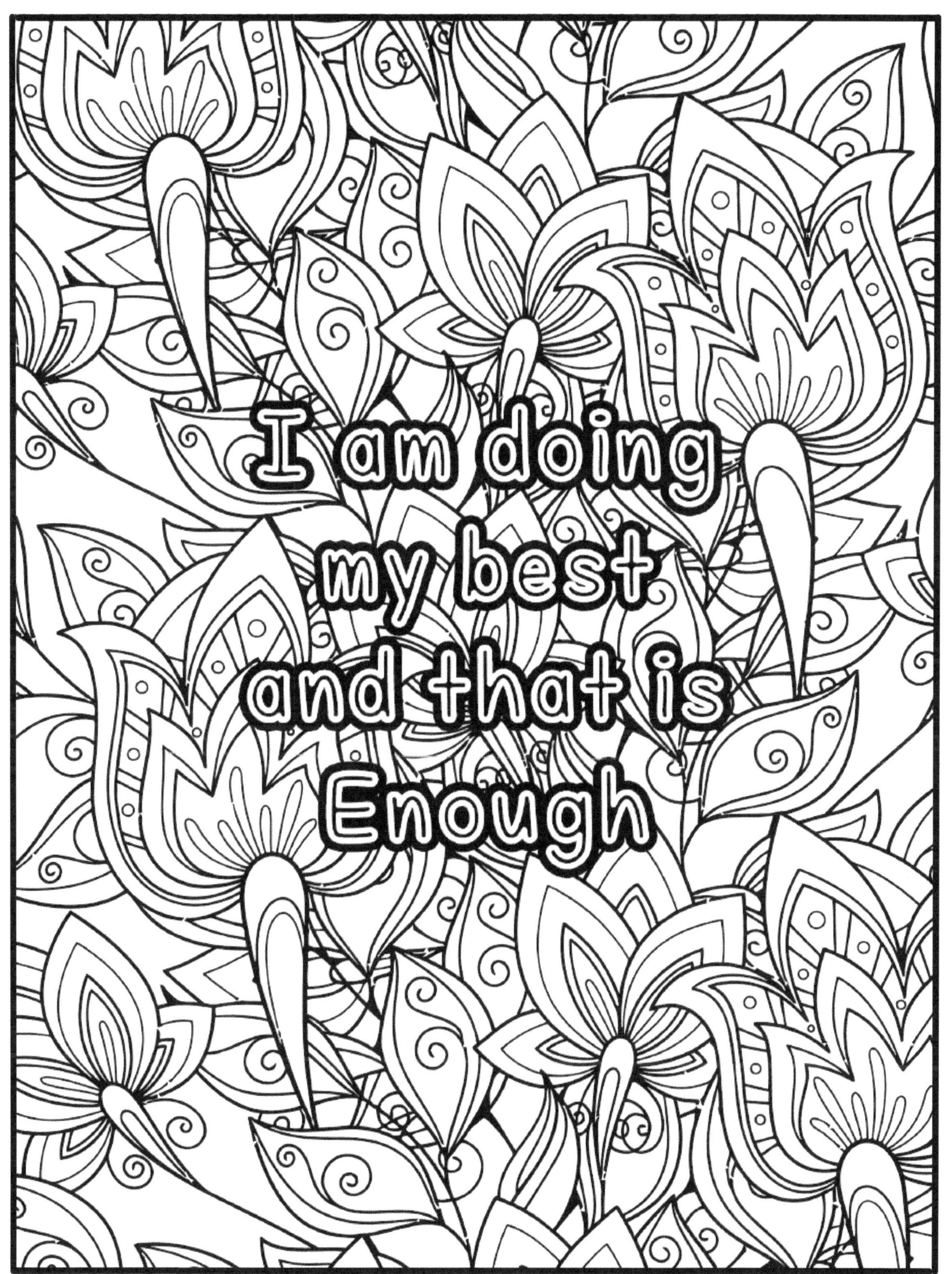

I am doing
my best
and that is
Enough

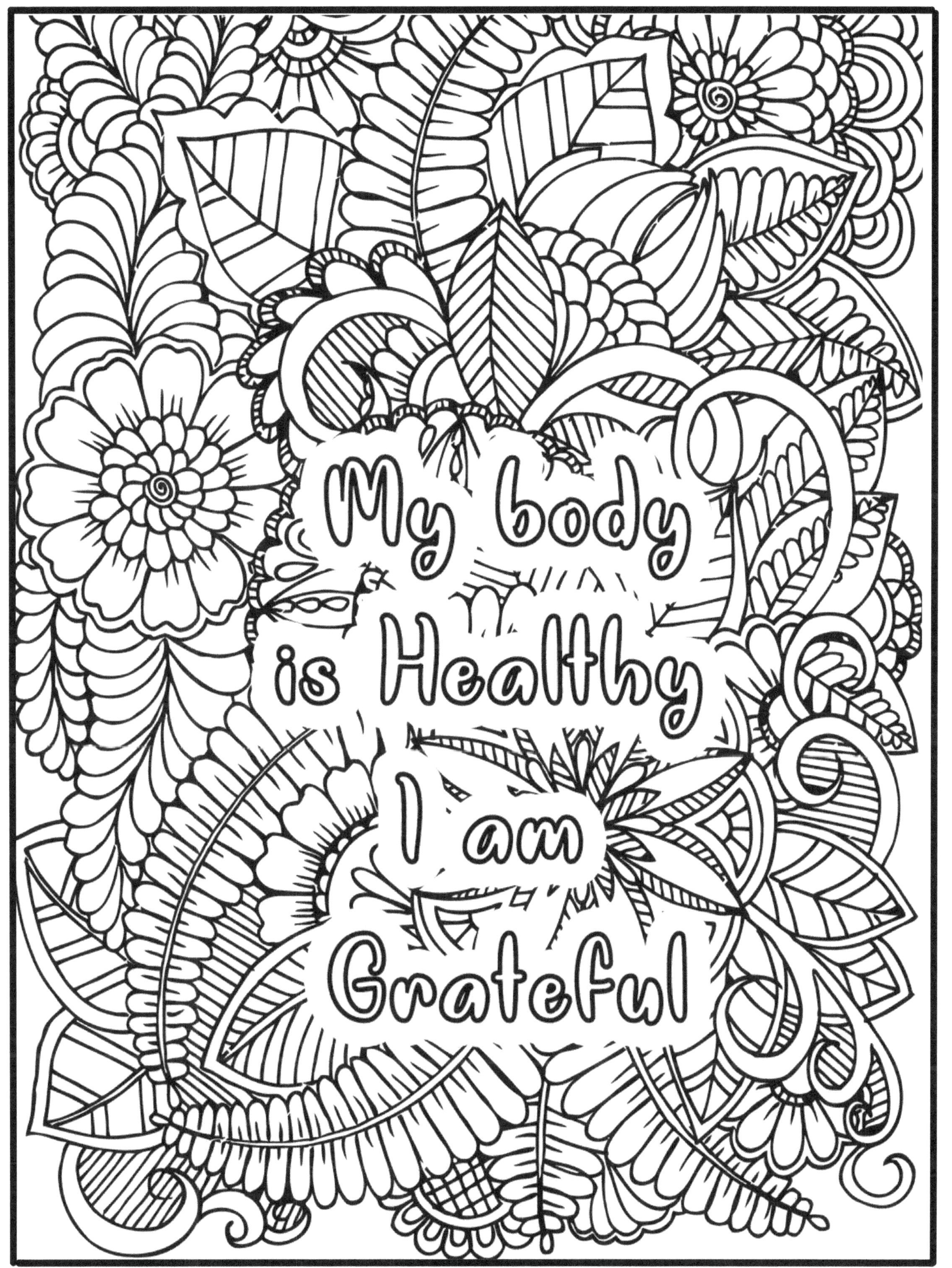
My body
is Healthy
I am
Grateful

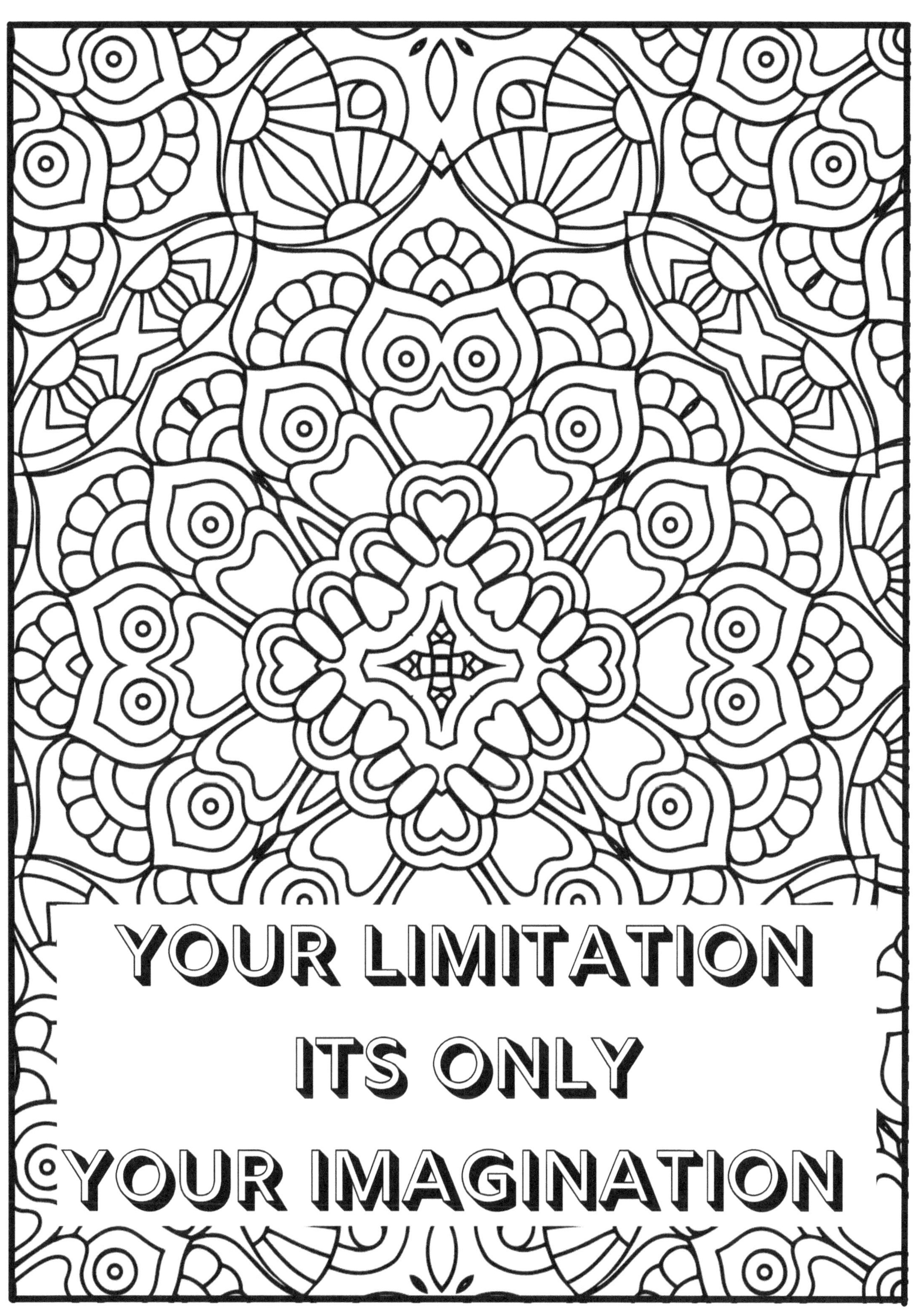

YOUR LIMITATION
ITS ONLY
YOUR IMAGINATION

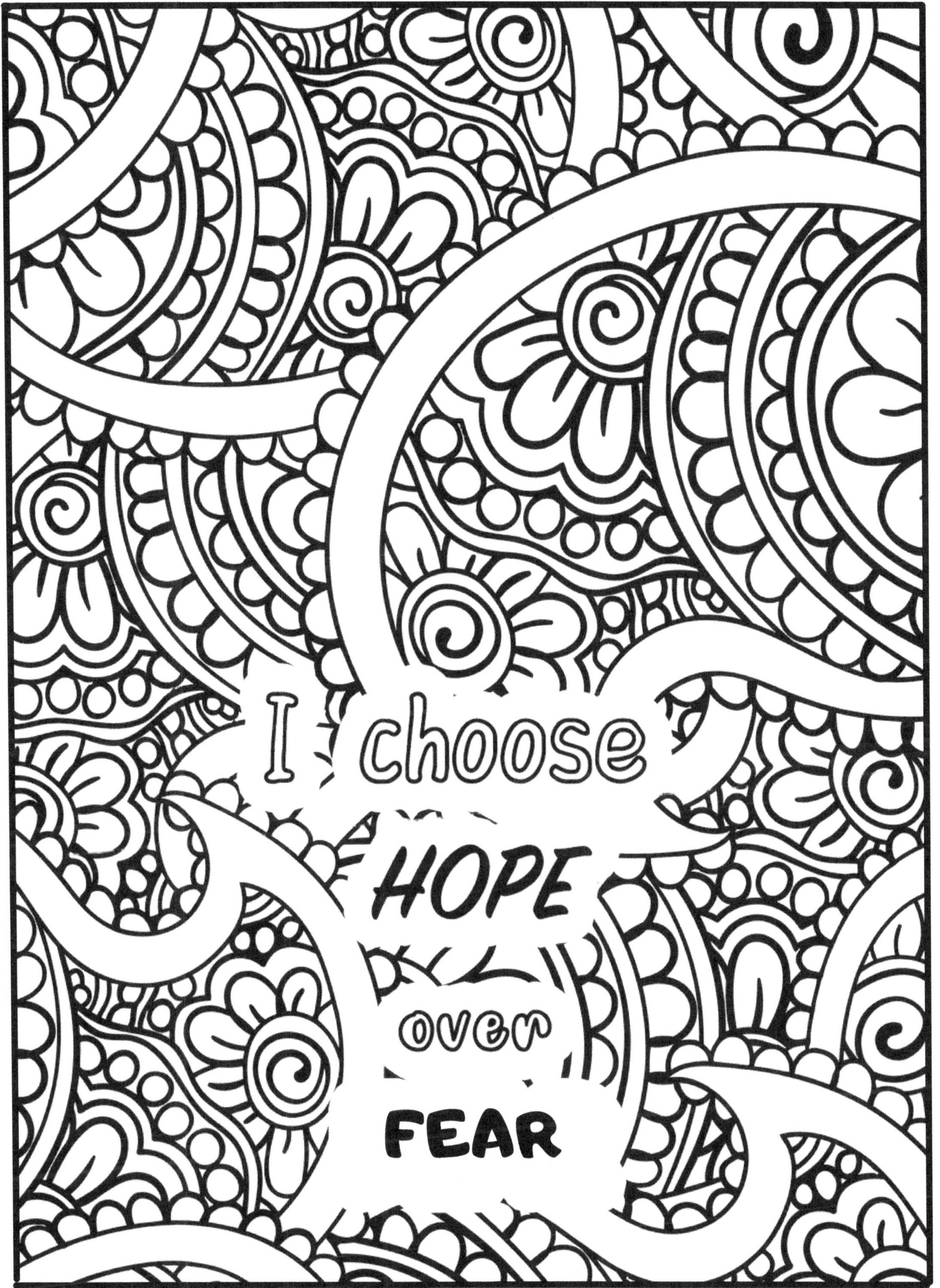

I choose
HOPE
over
FEAR

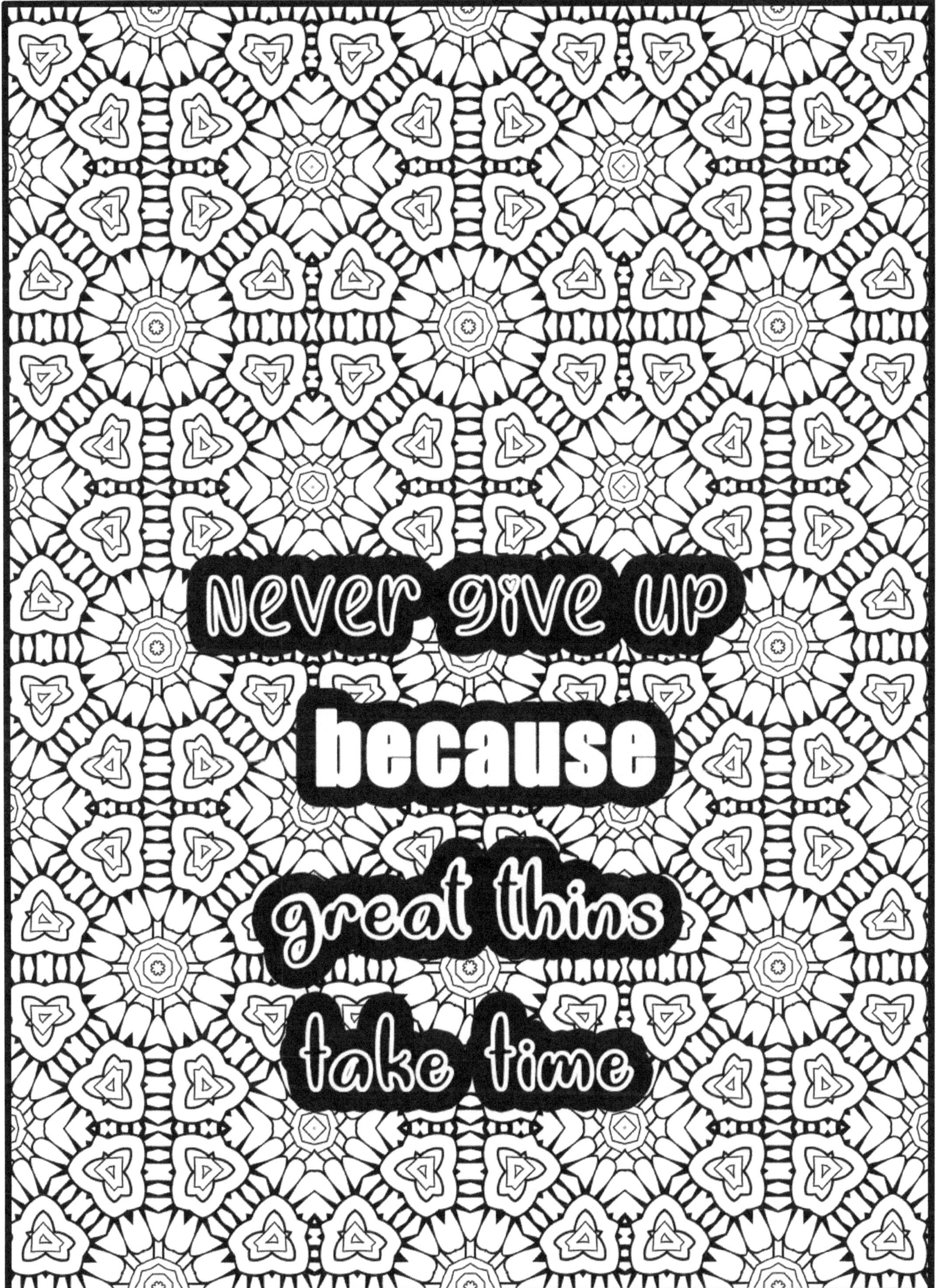

Never give up
because
great thins
take time

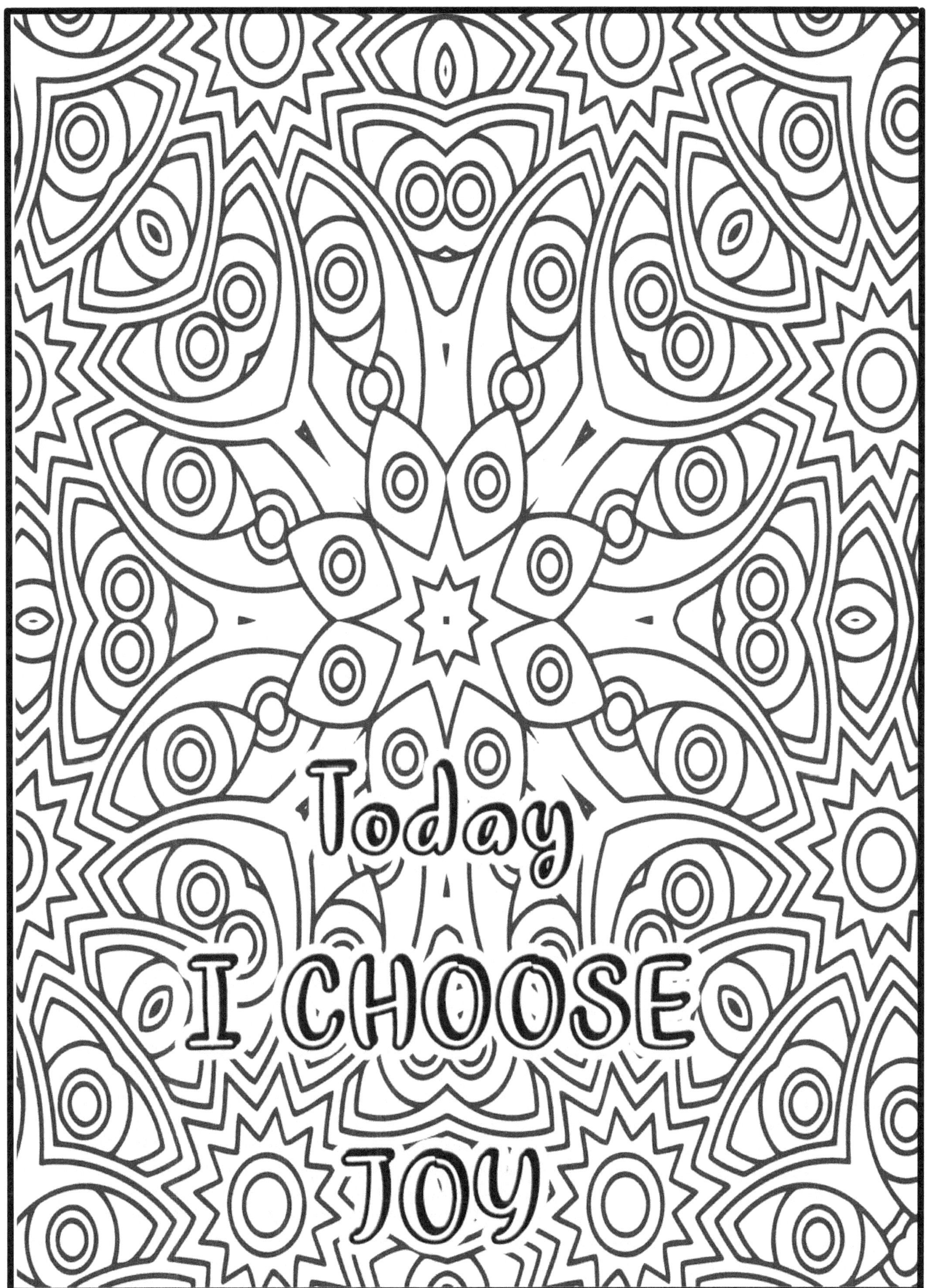

Today
I CHOOSE
JOY

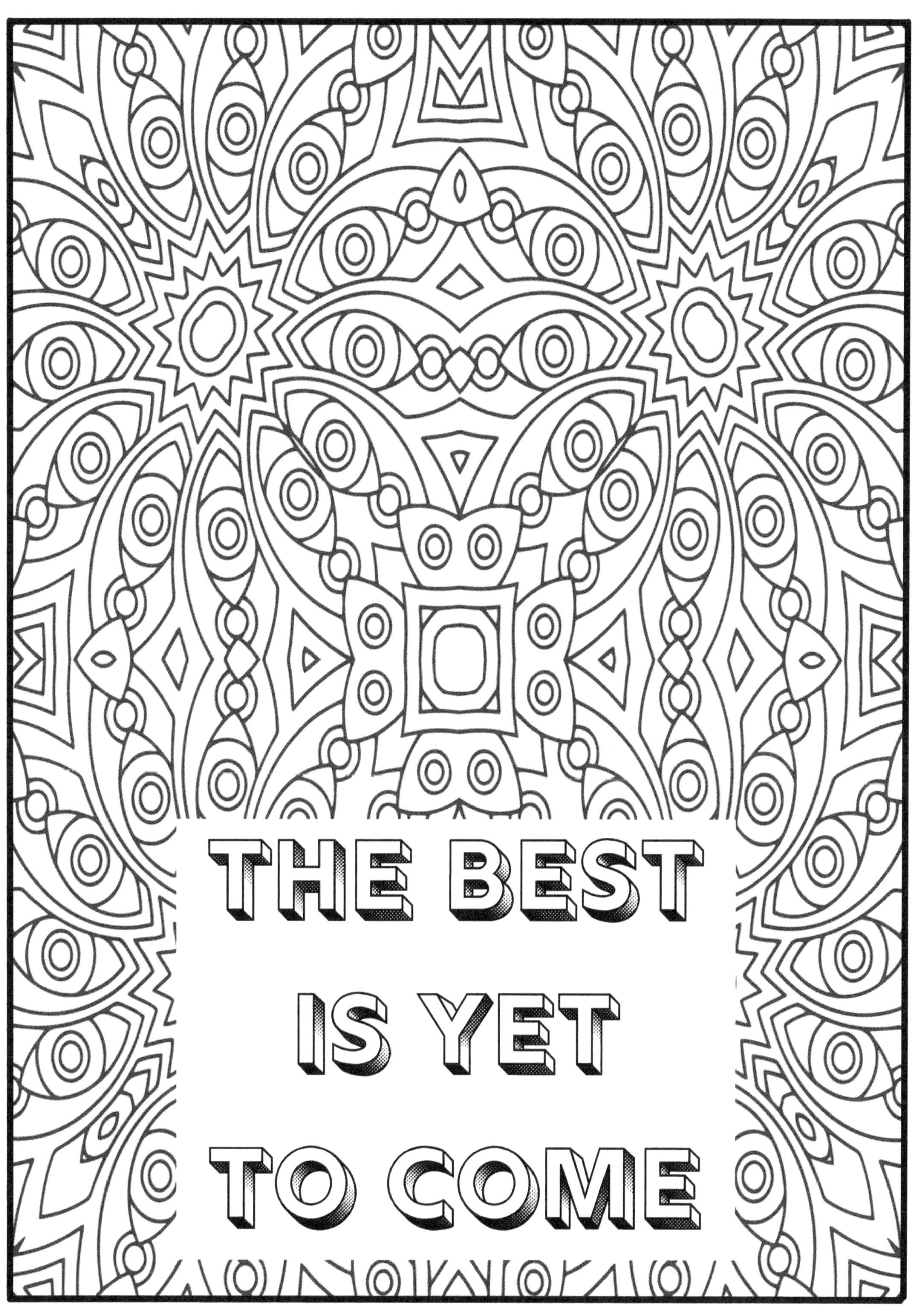

THE BEST
IS YET
TO COME

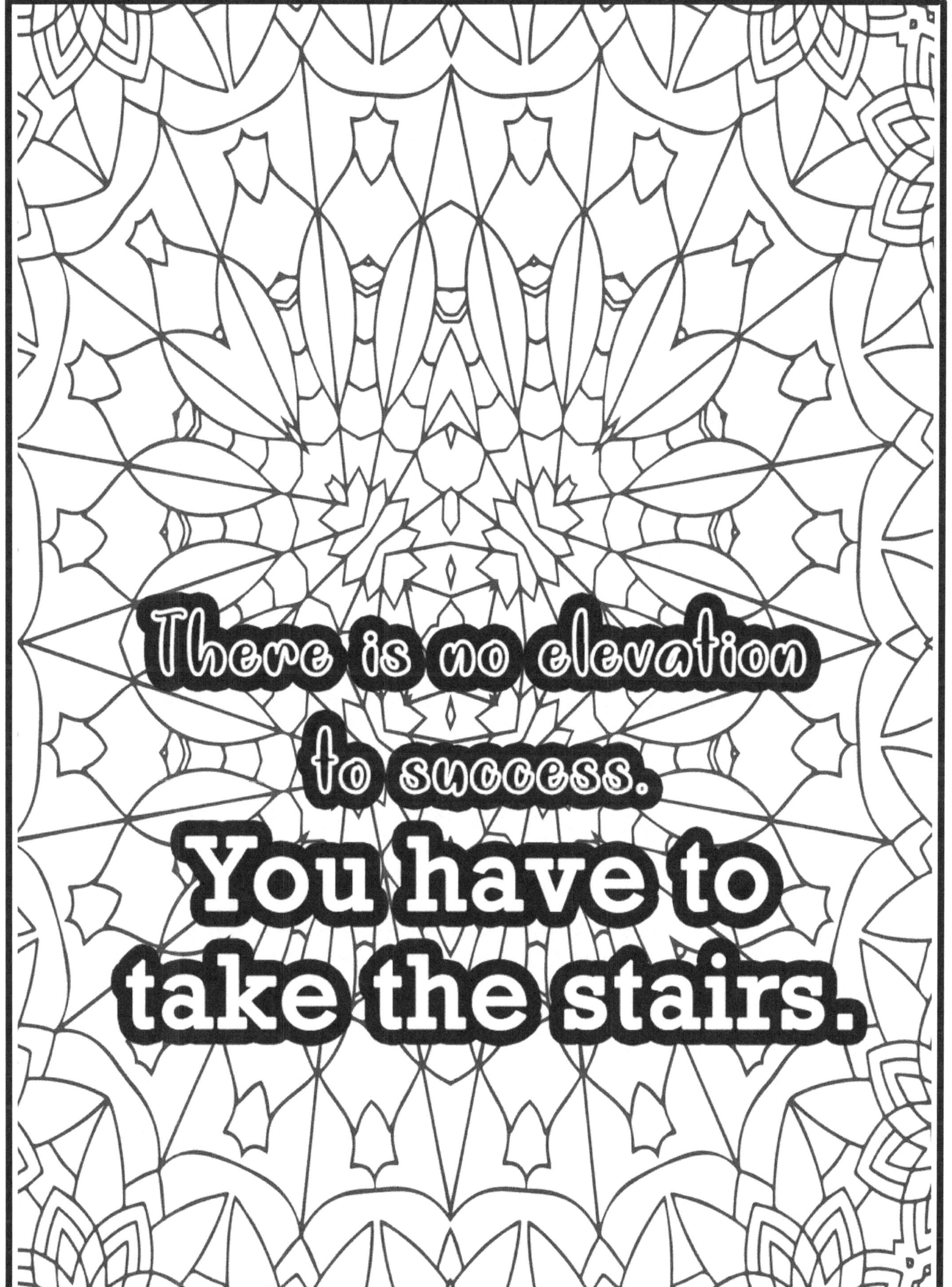
There is no elevation
to success.
You have to
take the stairs.

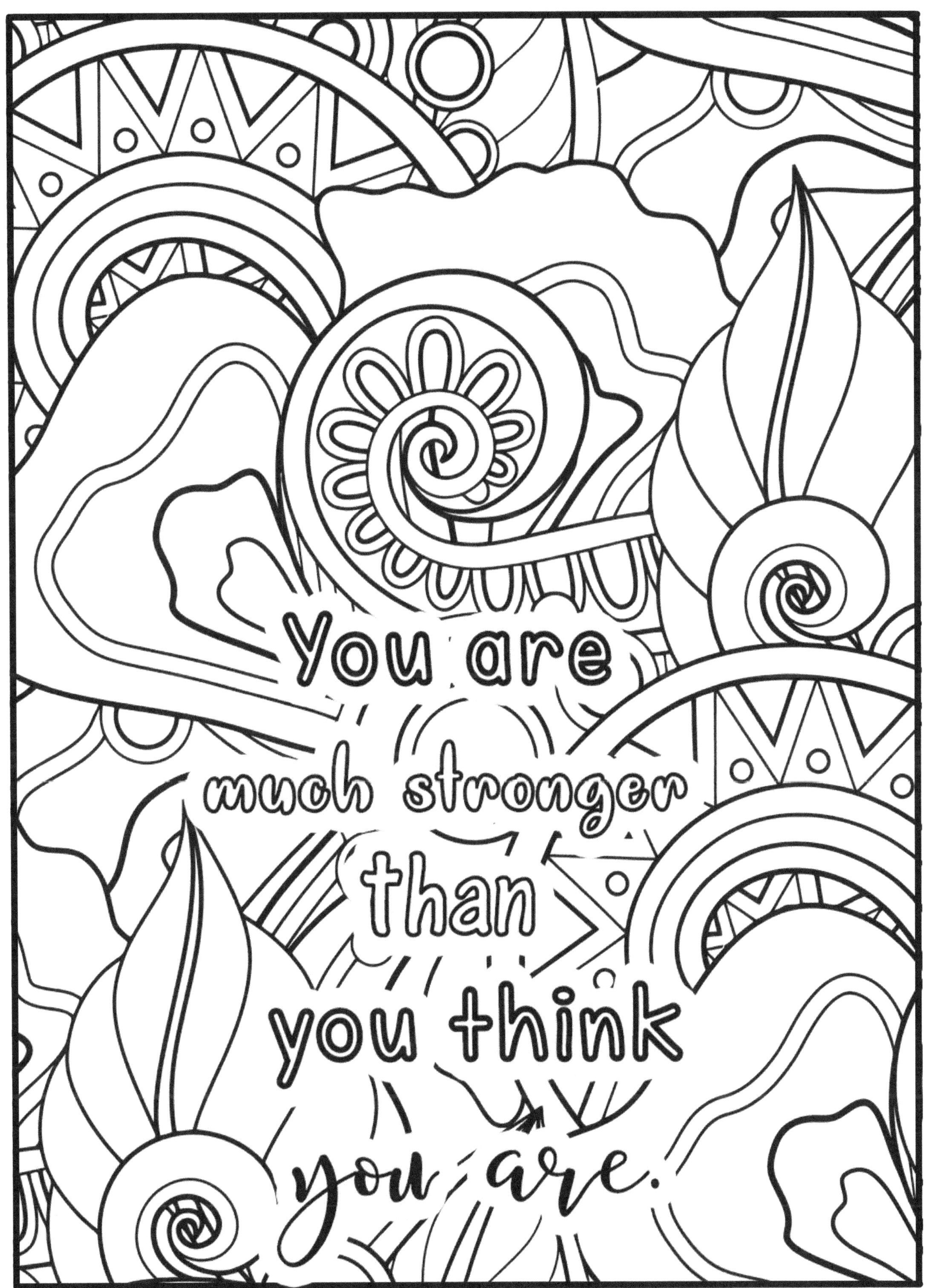

You are
much stronger
than
you think
you are.

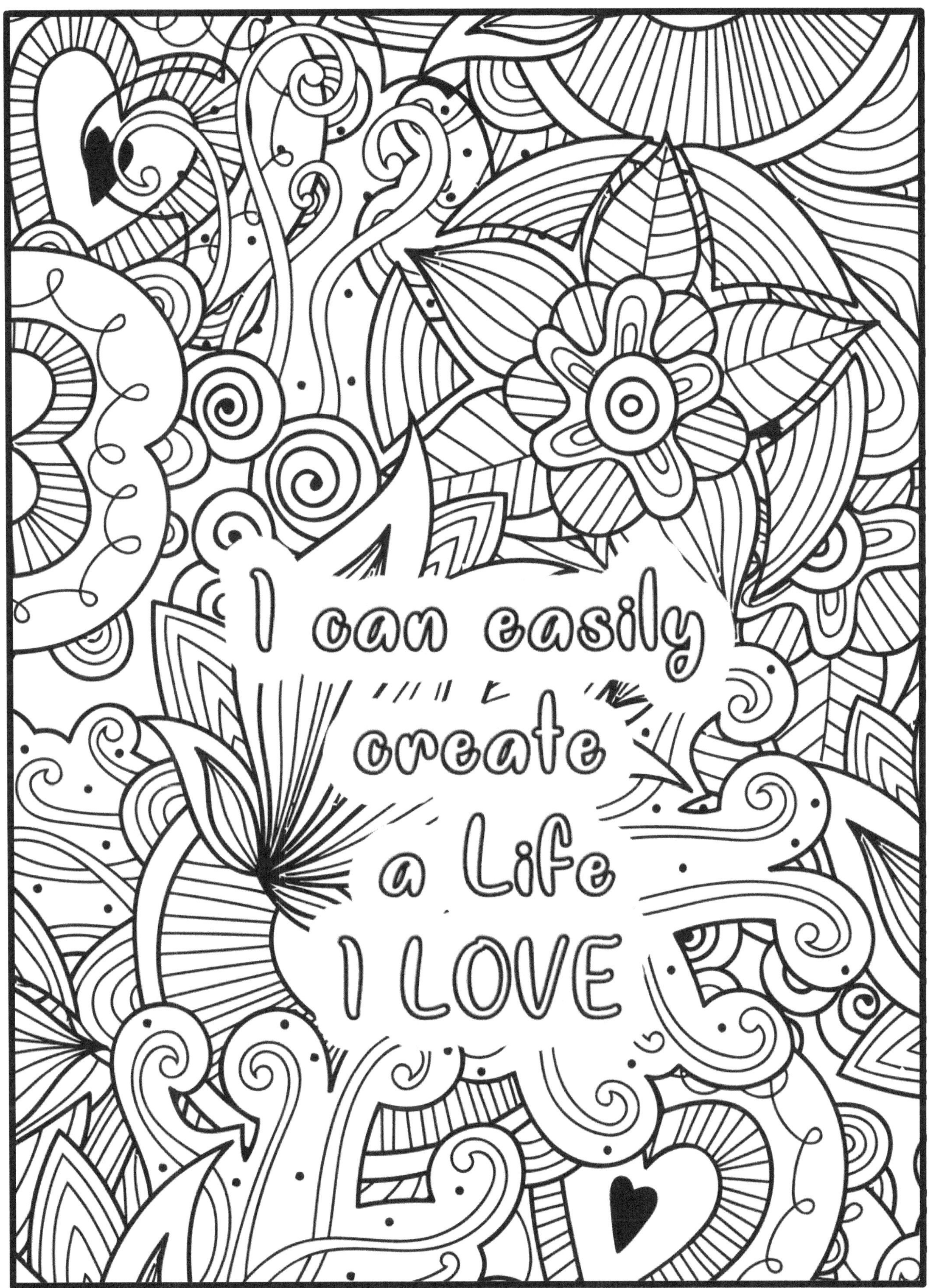
I can easily
create
a Life
I LOVE

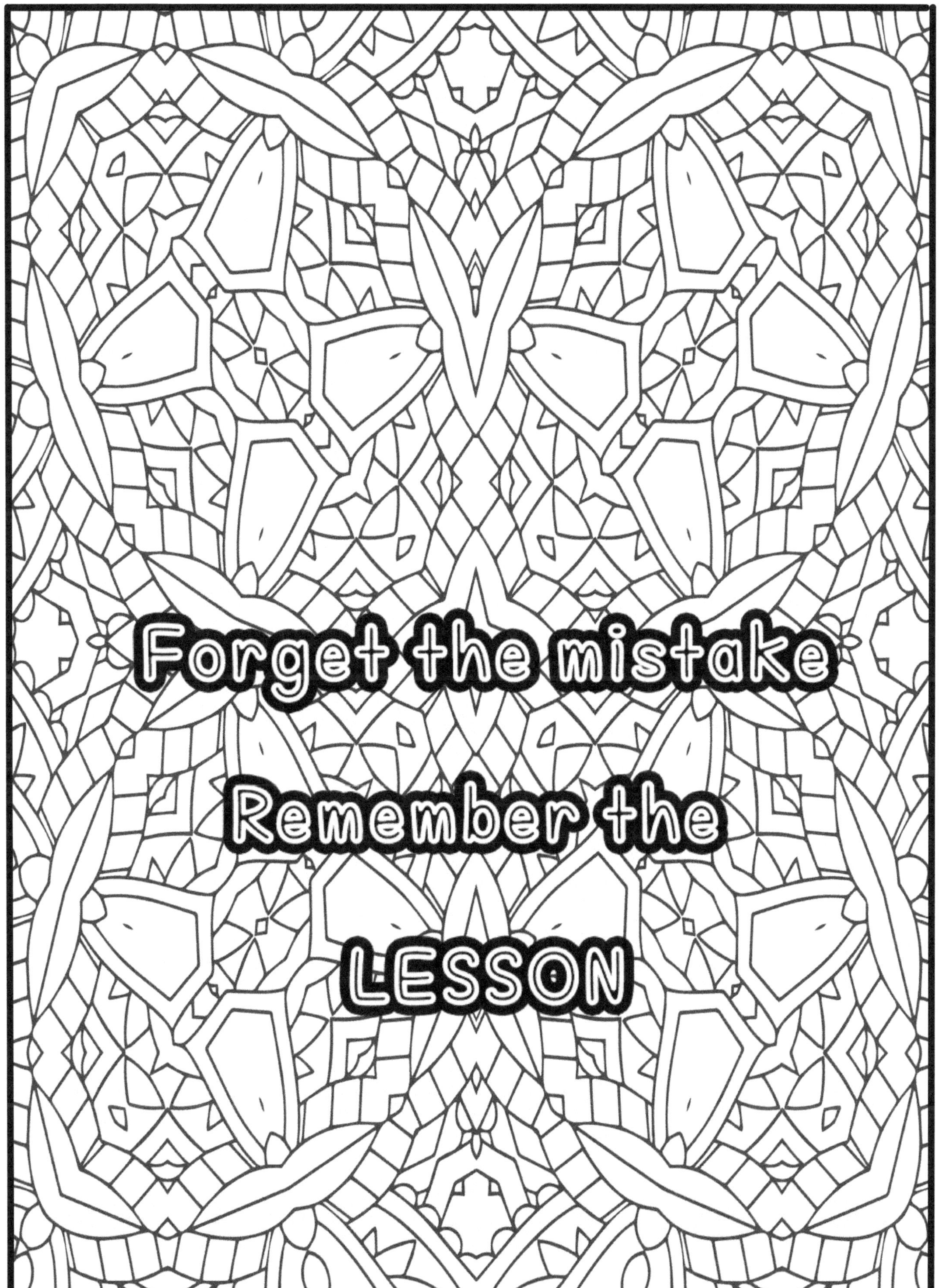

Forget the mistake
Remember the
LESSON

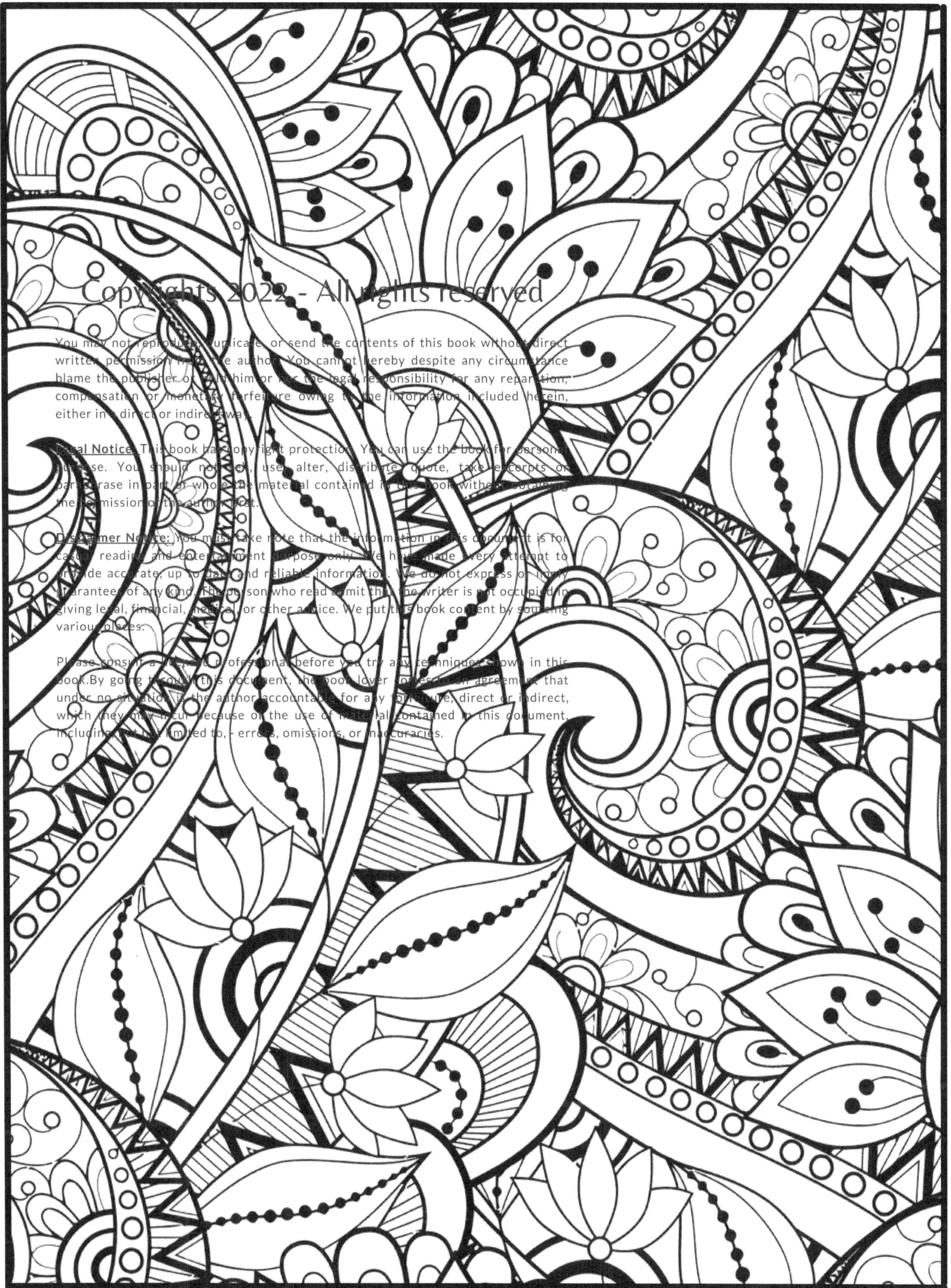

Thank you!

We hope you enjoyed our book.

As a small family company, your feedback is very important to us .

Please let us know how you like our book at :

pickme.readme@gmail.com

Copyrights 2022 - All rights reserved